Extraordinary News

for ordinary people

HEATH TRAMPE

Ⅲ Tri-Pillar Publishing

EXTRAORDINARY NEWS FOR ORDINARY PEOPLE

Tri-Pillar Publishing
Anaheim Hills, California
Website: www.TriPillarPublishing.com
E-mail: tripillarpublishing@cox.net

International Standard Book Number --13:   978-1-942654-03-2

International Standard Book Number --10:   1-942654-03-0

Library of Congress Catalog Card Number: 2009927927

First edition, June, 2009

Printed in the United States of America

Contents

To Aunnee, my rib.

Acknowledgments

A book might be compared to a sculpture. Whether or not the passing admirer can fully comprehend the creative process of the artist, the shape remains true. Books, as sculptures, are permanent reminders of the Muse within.

Many thanks are due to Harold Senkbeil, Renea Gernant, Charles Blanco, Bert Mueller, Chris LaBoube, David Kahle, and Kristen Larson. Without your willingness to take a chisel to my piece, it might have always remained an unrecognized dream.

To J. Brown, who inspired me to see the shape beneath the stone and steadied my hand throughout the process.

To Josephine Dibble and Tri-Pillar Publishing. You carried the biggest tools. You effected the most profound change. You helped me see the reality just under the surface. Your spirit and strength have inspired me to write – and to create – for the rest of my life.

To my family, who raised me to see the truth beyond my vision and the glory beyond this world. Nothing that is worthwhile ever comes without faith and sacrifice.

To Andrea, my wife. Without your constant love and devotion, I would not have had the will to push through late nights and countless hours of contemplation. This work is as much yours as it is mine.

Finally, to the One who breathed life into this dust, wept for my sins, and died so that I might live for eternity: thank You. This is for You. It's *all* for You.

8

Foreword

The twenty-first century has brought with it a world of wonderful technological advances and a virtual overload of information through vast media sources. Although these are delivered to society with the best of intentions, there arrives more on the serving tray than what appears at first glance. Certainly, new high-tech inventions and discoveries in science are making our lives more efficient and providing wonderful conveniences to enhance our day. However, we must consider the cloud which accompanies every silver lining. A downside of these so-called "advancements" in our society is, of course, the added pressures that people feel to achieve greater, more impressive heights of performance. We struggle to keep up with the latest and the greatest trends. A constant bombardment of information and advertising taunts us with ideals and standards that are just out of reach. It's no wonder that so many of us today feel a sense of dissatisfaction with our lives. Some of us even battle depression or harbor a sense of inferiority because we simply do not measure up to the new standard. Our culture is shouting a message: Ordinary is not good enough! The common and the usual are simply unacceptable.

Whatever happened to being content with living an ordinary life? Not that long ago, rising at the rooster's crow at the crack of dawn and blowing the candles out at the end of the evening sandwiched a long and laborious – but immensely rewarding – day on the farm. Men lived simply, laboring with their hands and playing checkers down at the general store in their free time. Wives made time to bake pies, tend to the garden, and create masterfully designed quilts and needlepoint. They crocheted mittens and scarves for their children. Whether or not you agree with the stereotypical gender roles that accompanied the days of yore, I believe that most will admit that there was a beauty and peace that came with living a simpler lifestyle, free from all of the clutter and hectic schedules that consume our daily lives.

What about the ordinary people? For those who may not be considered remarkable by the world's standards, or even exceptional in their own eyes, there is an important message awaiting you within the pages of this book. Author Heath Trampe is here to tell you the Good News... no, the EXTRAORDINARY NEWS – and it's for *all* people! Jesus Christ didn't die for only the elite of society. His sacrifice was for *everyone*. God's amazing gifts aren't just for the cleverest, the wisest, and the most highly skilled. He bestows His grace upon even those who are, by definition, commonplace. Finally, our Lord does not limit the privilege of sharing this Good News to only those who are quick with the tongue or eloquent with the pen. The honor is granted to even the simplest person to share the love and light of Christ. God works through ordinary people, and this is indeed extraordinary news!

Heath brings this very message to his readers in a way which is inspirational, informative, and also fun to read. His writing style flows well and allows the reader's eyes to glide across the pages like socks on a newly waxed floor. More so, the author has a knack for reading between the lines of Scripture and bringing to light many fascinating theological points and applications for everyday life, most of which cannot be easily recognized by a quick glance of the text. And yet, *Extraordinary News for Ordinary People* has something for everyone. There are many simple and straightforward concepts which are practical and functional, even for those seeking a lighter read. These concepts are interspersed with deep and contemplative insights which will edify even the most seasoned scholars. His conventional language and conversational approach to writing ensure that this is a book that everyone will enjoy.

Heath purposely chooses some of the lesser known characters in the Bible as his focus of study. He does this to show that even average individuals are used by God. This accomplishes two objectives. First, it gives the common man hope. If God works through even the regular people throughout history, then He can certainly work through those today whom society has labeled as nothing special. Run-of-the-mill people like us should lift our heads high, proclaiming: "Almighty God can use even me for His holy purposes!" Second, the weight is off of our shoulders. By using ordinary people to do His work, God is showing that all power and glory belong to Him alone. The work that we achieve for the Kingdom does not depend upon any strength from within ourselves. God will accomplish great things through us, in spite of ourselves. Praise be to God, whose love is shown in and for all of His precious children, even the ordinary ones.

Reverend J. Brown is a pastor at Praise Lutheran Church in Fort Wayne, Indiana. He is a 7th degree black belt and the founder of USA Martial Arts, a Christian based karate organization dedicated to sharing the love of Christ through martial arts. J. is also an author and has written multiple books, such as "Street Smarts from Christian Martial Arts" and "Breaking Barriers."

Introduction

Extraordinary News

This book is not a scholarly theological work, nor is it an autobiography. I've never done anything, made anything, or said anything that would make me famous or even well recognized by anyone. I'm an ordinary guy, and I write this for all of the other ordinary men and women who may or may not know that there's something more to this life. If you're like I was, you've been trying to find that "something more" for some time now, and quite unsuccessfully. Perhaps one thing or another gives you a temporary release from the daily grind of life, but soon you find yourself back where you started, feeling miserable and hollow. Our bookshelves are full of self-help titles, but even these step-by-step guides for life leave us unsatisfied. Their purpose is to prove that we are not as adept at fixing our own lives as the one who wrote the book. They almost invariably achieve this purpose. Some-times self-help techniques *can* benefit us temporarily, but this improvement is usually similar to a New Year's resolution. After awhile it becomes a hassle to change our lifestyle or to try things on our own, and we become discouraged and quit.

You must realize that you're not in control of everything that happens in your life. Wanting something badly enough or working your hardest doesn't always result in attaining that which you desire. Only by stepping back and taking a look at your life can you see that you really haven't been in the driver's seat at all. Your best efforts have failed because you cannot do anything of your own volition. God, the same Father, Son, and Holy Spirit who created the world and continues to sustain it, is the One who calls the shots.

God can simply be a part of your life – perhaps for an hour on Sunday morning – or He can be the very center of your life, every moment of every day. Once you've experienced His Holy Word in the Bible and have been called by the Holy Spirit to become a believer, you will begin to see that things have been provided for you all along. Comfort, confidence, love, and even eternal life are yours to receive, but only if you realize that they don't come from within you; they're gifts from God, and completely external.

We are all sinners in need of a Savior, and no one is exempt: *"**All** have sinned and fall short of the glory of God, and are justified freely by his grace through the redemption that came by Christ Jesus"* (Romans 3:23-24). Indeed, without Christ none of us would be able to stand before God's judgment throne. His grace changes everything. Most of us will experience a time in our lives when this spiritual truth finally hits home for us in a powerful, deeply personal way. It certainly did for me, and I would like to share my story with you. Therefore, the next few pages are a piece of my own life, and I sincerely hope that my own imperfect experience can bring you to the realization that still brings new things to light for me each day: Jesus Christ is my Lord and my life.

Ordinary Beginnings

The 17th of June was a very ordinary day to be born in a very ordinary hospital in the very ordinary town of Kearney, Nebraska. I was neither small nor large as a baby, born into a middle class family trying to make a living as farmers. While farming is among the noblest of professions, it rarely provides for a lucrative lifestyle. However, since my entire community was comprised of these same salt-of-the-earth pioneers, I never pondered an existence beyond the curtain of corn.

Indeed I was quite satisfied until one day, much to my surprise, my family decided to move away from the farm. My dad was one of many farmers who left his land due to an offer of a free college education if he was willing to attempt another trade. He went to technical school, where his keen intelligence and athleticism earned him a job climbing radio towers for repairs, among many other tasks – a job that he kept into his 50's. My mom has worked many jobs to keep our family settled and comfortable. From bookkeeping to secretarial work, she has been my dad's right arm in financial and family affairs. The reason I'm sharing these details with you is to show you how ordinary I truly am. I grew up without much more than my family and the love they provided. We were regular people, making the best life we could for ourselves, and although my family boasted a steady church attendance, even this rendered us quite ordinary in our small religious community.

Living in the conservative, Christian center of America, we always went to church, and I just assumed that everyone else did also. All of the kids in my school went to one church or another: some were Roman Catholic, while others were Lutherans or Methodists. Even in the small town where I went to school and spent most of my childhood (Amherst, Nebraska, pop. 250), we had several churches brimming with parishioners. A short trip down the road provided access to just about any kind of church you can think of, all of them full of devout, hard-working Nebraskans. As children, my brother and I never questioned why we were in church or talked much about our religion; it was just another part of our lives that neither demanded nor required much thought. Although I continued to go to church services as I entered into my adulthood, my faithful attendance was due more to the perceived expectations of my parents than anything else. At one point, I actually thought the entire Christian existence revolved around paying one's dues to God and man by going to church every Sunday. It was a "sit in the pew and God will forgive you" mentality, and in my own mind, it gave me a purpose for warming the bench each week.

As a child, sitting in the church service was one of my least favorite times during the week. I can look back now and see the *true* beauty of my little church, but while I was growing up, it was just the place with the hard wooden benches that made my rear end fall asleep. My own uncle was the pastor of my church for many years, and even though I liked him outside of church, I thought he was pretty boring when I had to sit and listen to one of his sermons (which were actually very good). Singing hymns was bearable, but all of the dialogue between the pastor and the people seemed unnecessary and tedious to an impatient young man such as myself. Heaven forbid that there be Communion or a Baptism, which would prolong the church service by as much as twenty extra minutes on a given Sunday. I wanted to hurry and get out of there so that my family could make our reservations at Pizza Hut. Thus was my life as a Christian youth.

At this point Jesus was just a picture in the hallway or a smiling cartoon character in a Sunday school lesson. I never actually read the Bible or listened when it was being read in church. Sure, I knew the names of Solomon, Jonah, Jesus, Zacchaeus and many more of the famous people talked about in the Bible, but I didn't care to learn who they *really* were. They were simply ancient people in a boring book that didn't seem relevant to my life. My primary worries of the time were which of my friends I could sit with during the service, and how much mischief we could get away with before we got into trouble – which, as it turns out, wasn't much.

This was my life, and there appeared to be nothing extraordinary about it. I was merely one of the guys, occupying the same social circle from the time I was five until I graduated from high school. Of course, this doesn't mean that my life was easy – quite the contrary. I may have gone to high school with all of my oldest friends, but it would prove to be the most challenging four years of my life.

Girls, Football, and Being a Nerd

Amherst Public School was (and still is) a K-12 institution. This means that I went to school with the same group of kids (about 25 in my class) from the time I entered kindergarten until I received my high school diploma. One might think that this environment would feel very comfortable to me, when in all actuality entering high school simply meant that I had more bullies to deal with. Due to the 20-30 pounds of extra weight that I could never seem to lose, I was considered the fat kid in my class. Instead of leaving me alone, a few individuals made their educational experience complete by repeatedly destroying my self-esteem for nearly a decade. When you have 25 students in your class, it's not possible to simply hang out with a new group of kids and escape the abuse. You have to directly face each humiliating moment, knowing that almost every person in the school is aware of your plight. In spite of this, even when it may have been easier to hide my grief in seclusion, I made the bold decision to go out for football my freshman year, where I received the most beautiful collection of bruises you've ever seen. As much as I enjoyed the daily beatings, I soon traded in my football pads for a pair of running shoes.

Perhaps I should mention that I come from a running family. My dad is a talented and very serious long distance runner. Our refrigerator and walls are adorned with awards and recognitions of past achievements, and there's always a Runner's World magazine in the bathroom. I immediately saw cross-country as a way to connect with my father a little more. Unfortunately, I had very little going for me in the realm of natural athletic talent. My only experience with running a mile in junior high had been extremely embarrassing. I was running in dead last by such an incredible margin that they were setting up for the next race, thinking that my full competitive speed was a warm-up jog! The officials had to announce to everyone that I was still running and that the track needed to be cleared until all of the runners were done with the race. Now *that's* slow!

Although neither of the high school cross country teams at my school was very competitive in the meets, something remarkable happened. Even though we comprised a rather motley crew of runners, we made some lasting friendships, and for the first time we were having a lot of fun in our sport. The pressures surrounding football and volleyball didn't apply to us. Our coach was more interested in improving our fitness and self-confidence than he was in winning meets. We had a lot more fun than the teams who were competitive, because we were participating for pure enjoyment. Not every aspect of it was a complete thrill ride, such as the six mile runs on hilly country roads in humid 98 degree weather, but on the whole it was simply magical.

I eventually found myself as Amherst's number one runner, and I was even medaling in some of the smaller meets. However, another thing happened that year – I became extremely arrogant. The meager successes that I enjoyed on the cross country courses and in practice went directly to my head. I was still awkward and a little overweight, but I was trimming down fast. With this new physique came a different self-perception and I had no intentions of being a doormat for the rest of my life.

My senior year of high school would also produce one of the greatest things ever to happen to me: my very first girlfriend, Andrea. In the beginning we were just set up to go to the prom together, but a love soon blossomed. To tell the complete story of Andrea and Heath would require many more pages, so suffice it to say that we were smitten with each other. After four years of not fitting in or finding a niche, I was finally an athlete with a girlfriend, and I was going off to college! I was determined not to make the same mistakes that I had regretted from high school, even if it meant a complete overhaul of my former personality.

Running, Dating, and Finding a Niche

Although I was in excellent physical shape and willing to work hard, the cross country coach at the university that I was attending dissuaded me from trying out for his squad. He had seven solid runners, and didn't have any interest in someone who wouldn't make an immediate impact. I even bested his qualifying time trial, but he still told me that I couldn't be on his team. Thus, I didn't run for the university my freshman year of college, but trained diligently on my own, sometimes for hours each day. When that coach was let go the following season, I decided to finally try out for the team. A few preseason workouts revealed that I might, to my extreme delight, be one of the school's best runners. This day marked the start of my new life as a competitive runner. While I went on dates and hung out with friends and even received good grades in my classes in the years that followed, I only noticed my running. I was greedy, training harder in the off-season than I should have, and eventually broke my foot in the process. If you're wondering what was going on in my spiritual life at that time and why I haven't mentioned it, it's because spirituality and Jesus Christ were unimportant to me. Running was my god.

I started attending Andrea's church right after high school, mostly just to be around her. My body had a wonderful attendance rating, but my mind never came; it was too busy thinking about the next workout or physical therapy session. Surprisingly, I prayed quite a bit during this time. Every night, I prayed that God would heal my foot, strengthen my body, and allow me to win races. Instead of thanking God for the good things in my life, I made a list of demands each night. This was my relationship with my Heavenly Father. When my fractured foot finally healed, I was a road warrior once again, racing nearly every weekend. I won almost every time, sometimes by several minutes, but I had turned my back on Christ. I wouldn't let myself become an "ordinary" guy ever again. I sought to change everything about myself, including my religious image. I wasn't bold enough to quit going to church, just enough to quit caring. As proof of my new image, I also joined a fraternity that year.

Joining a fraternity was my way of shedding my weak and vulnerable past. Some of the guys were really nice, intelligent, and conscientious. I don't mean to put those individuals down, but the reality is that most of them were the same mean-spirited bullies that made my life miserable in high school. I paid my dues on time, lived in the fraternity house, and brought the house GPA up, so most of them treated me with a sort of mild tolerance. I spent most of my time in my dorm room, thinking about running and picturing myself on top of the world. And then, one evening, my nearsighted view of life changed in the blink of an eye.

I was serving alcohol at one of the parties that my fraternity attended/hosted. I served *way* too much, not caring at all how it might affect the recipients. One of those people, a friend of mine, went to bed that night completely intoxicated and fell from the top bunk in his dorm room, landing eye socket first on the desk below. He was permanently injured, both physically and mentally. As I watched my drunken fraternity brothers stumbling around and trying to get him some medical attention, I was sickened to my very core. Countless questions ran through my mind. Had I contributed to this horrible event? What direction was my life going? I couldn't take the "what-ifs" that were haunting me night after night. I had to get away from this destructive environment as soon as possible.

With God's strength, although I wouldn't have given Him much of the credit, I started making some changes. I moved out of the fraternity house during the semester break, got an apartment with a cross-country teammate, and made plans to transfer schools. I ended up picking, somewhat at random, Concordia University in Seward, Nebraska, which is a Lutheran school. Little did I know that this would prove to be one of the most positive decisions I've ever made. Unfortunately, my transfer didn't begin so smoothly.

In face to face interactions, the men's and women's cross country teams seemed to like me a lot. I was even contributing towards an almost perfect season of team victories. At first I thought everything was just fine, but I quickly discovered that I was mistaken. My cocky demeanor and quick tongue worked well as defense mechanisms at my former school, but now I seemed to be attracting the wrong sort of attention. Fights would start up for what I thought to be no reason, and I was constantly on someone's bad list. I began to wonder if I was in the right place or if I *could* make friends anywhere I went.

When I arrived at Concordia, my attitude stunk. I hardly ever went to the daily chapel services, and I attempted to distance myself from all religious functions. Even though I would have been the top runner at my last college, in Concordia's superior program I was middle of the pack. *Average*! I was forced to be ordinary in the one thing that I

felt defined me as extraordinary, and it burned.   My
roommate was faster than me, and I took my jealousy and
frustration out on him whenever I could.   I found so many
faults with the guy that by the end of the year we were barely
speaking to each other.   During that first year after the
transfer, I couldn't tell if I had one true friend among my
classmates.   In reality, I had many good friends, but I wasn't
reciprocating the gesture.   When Spring Break of my junior
year came around, I was ready to go home and bury my grief
in seclusion.   My family still supported me, and they were
always there for me, even when nobody else was.   The last
person I wanted to see was Andrea, and I figured that she felt
the same about me.

Snagged by the Lord

I was driving home for break and listening to my
"Jesus Christ Superstar" soundtrack when something profound happened.   As I was listening to the actor playing
Jesus sing in the Garden of Gethsemane, I broke down crying.
There were many times throughout that year on my commute
home that I had broken down before, seriously considering
whether I should just roll my car and end it all.   This time it
was different.   I now realized something that I had never fully
understood before.   The words in the Bible were completely
my own, a personal message for me and my life.   Waves of
shock jolted through me as everything that I had ever heard
about Jesus Christ rushed to the forefront of my mind, and I
was overcome with the sensation.   I felt like I was taking my
first gasp of fresh air after nearly drowning.   I began to truly
realize that my pain and grief were nothing compared to those
of Christ, who chose to save me and all mankind through His
death on the cross and His glorious resurrection.   At the time
I didn't know what to do with these thoughts and emotions,

but they gave me an unquenchable thirst to learn more about the God that I had ignored for most of my life. In the week that followed, I also met with Andrea and we talked for hours about our past and future. From that very moment in the car, the Lord took hold and began to lead me. The scales had fallen from my eyes. Every seed of God's Word that had ever been planted within me grew into a very real and unwavering faith in Jesus Christ. I even decided to change my major and become a pastor, although it was little more than a dream at that point. What a week!

I went back to school and realized that I had wronged most of my friends, although I had some difficulty making amends right away. It's hard to sweep away months of damage in a few weeks. But a surprising thing happened. I talked to some of my classmates about my desire to become a pastor and, much to my surprise, they were overjoyed with the idea. I figured that they'd be condescending or hold my wicked deeds and shallow character in front of me as a barrier to such an honorable office. Neither happened. I was so elated by their encouragement and support that I even approached the pre-Seminary director on campus, whom I had never even met before, but who would soon become a close and trusted mentor. My future was in God's hands – as it always had been!

Things really started happening from that point forward. In May of that year, I asked for Andrea's hand in marriage. She'd seen such a change in me that she confidently said yes. I also attempted to make amends with everyone I had hurt over the past few years. Most of them were very glad to see this change in my attitude, and welcomed me back with open arms. The prodigal son was coming home.

My senior year of college was a whirlwind of important events, self-reflection, and positive change. My philosophy toward running underwent a major transformation as well. Personal achievement didn't matter as much as it had before, and helping my team became my number one running priority. Ironically, that season was filled with my crowning athletic achievements. Not only did I help our team win the Conference Championship (the second time for CU in 30 years) and the Regional Championship, but also I was a major contributor for the Bulldogs at the NAIA National Championships. I finally accepted the fact that I was my own type of ordinary and realized that being "ordinary" is actually pretty great. I gained a surprising amount of respect from my teammates and, even more importantly, I made some lifelong friends. Now it was time to graduate and to say a reluctant farewell to my beloved home in Seward.

Upon graduating Summa Cum Laude from Concordia University, I went back home and married my high school sweetheart. I then proceeded to take her 13 hours away from all of her family and friends to Concordia Theological Seminary in Fort Wayne, Indiana. After three years of intense and life-changing pastoral formation, we accepted an assignment to serve the Lutheran Church in Latvia (LELB) as Long Term Missionaries. As for my passion for running, it is something that I now do for fitness and enjoyment. It will never take over my life again. I win all of my victories for the Lord, and serving God is my true purpose in life. Soon I'll become ordained and receive the title of Pastor, which means Shepherd. I'll tend to the flocks of the Good Shepherd, and I'll preach Christ Crucified for the rest of my life. If I did nothing else during my time on earth except preach the Good News of my Savior, I'd consider it a life well lived and a calling that I could never deserve.

Christ's Love for You

I have shared the story of my life with you because there's an important message here that I would like to convey. I never did anything to seek the Lord, although many around me were a constant witness. I certainly didn't think that I was worthy to be a leader and a shepherd of God's people. I knew nothing but seclusion and masks to hide my true self. Only two saw beyond those masks: my wife Andrea and, more importantly, my Lord and Savior Jesus Christ. Both of them loved me even when I was screaming at them to stop, and neither ever gave up on me. We don't all have "Andreas" in our lives, but we all have Christ. He's constantly vigilant over His flock, and when one goes astray, He'll come after it by any means necessary: **"He tends his flock like a shepherd: He gathers the lambs in his arms and carries them close to his heart; he gently leads those that have young"** (Isaiah 40:11).

The definition of a Christian isn't someone who goes to church and donates time and money to charity; it's someone who believes in Christ Crucified for the forgiveness of all of their sins. As a sinner, I know only too well what I deserve: an eternity in Hell. Maybe you've never done the kinds of rotten things that I have in my life, or perhaps you've done even worse. I'm here to tell you that Christ is greater than all of your sins, and He desires for you to walk with Him. From one "ordinary" person to another, I encourage you to keep listening to the message of life offered in the Bible and from your pastor at church. Only God knows the ways of the Holy Spirit, and He could work at any time in your heart and in your life. He'll guide you to realize that the message of the Bible is your own, and that Christ died for you. He knew that you would be a sinner incapable of fulfilling God's law from birth, and He sacrificed Himself for you anyway: **"I am the good shepherd; I know my sheep and my sheep know Me – just as the Father knows me and I know the Father – and I lay down my life for the sheep"** (John 10:14-15). He did this so that it wouldn't matter that you aren't perfect, because you're made perfect in Him. Always remember that God chooses ordinary men and women for His purposes. We are all His children.

In an effort to reinforce this point, I've compiled a list of twelve men and women in the Bible who were, by most standards, the very definition of average; but all were led to do remarkable things. From Biblical times to today, God works miracles in the meekest of His children. You have seen by now that I'm an example of this love. If I learned anything from my time at the seminary, it was that the majority of Christians are regular, average folks just like you and me. Our calling is a very high one, and one that we're certainly not worthy of. However, what we understand, and what the unbeliever needs to understand, is this: Christ died and rose again for *you*! When God looks upon your life, He sees Christ's perfection and your sin is no more. What comfort! What joy! And this has been true throughout time. As you read through the inspirational tales of these twelve men and women, try to see yourself in their characters, in their life situations, and in the way they are truly blessed to be children of God.

Jonah

³ Jonah ran away from the LORD and headed for Tarshish. He went down to Joppa, where he found a ship bound for that port. After paying the fare, he went aboard and sailed for Tarshish to flee from the LORD. (Jonah 1:3)

Almost anyone who has ever heard of Jonah knows that he was swallowed by a big fish. If that's the case, we should be far more interested in the abnormally large fish than in the man who became its dinner! Despite this, God has deemed Jonah worthy of his own book in the Bible, a book which is very short and starts with a bang. Instead of getting Jonah's background information, we hear only of his mission. A personal call from the Lord to preach against Nineveh doesn't make Jonah sound like an ordinary guy. However, his response to such a high calling strikes us as quite ordinary. **"But Jonah ran away from the LORD and headed for Tarshish"** (Jonah 1:3). Jonah figured that if he ran away from the situation, it might just blow over without involving him. Just imagine being told to go and preach to a quarter of a million people, only to tell them that they are damned sinners and that God is angry with them! However, one of the amazing characteristics of our Lord is that He never gives up on us, even when we've long since given up on Him.

Jonah hops[1] on a boat and escapes one situation only to find himself in another. Now he has to deal with the elements: **"such a violent storm arose that the ship**

---

[1] In an effort to bring these ancient Biblical characters to life in the mind of the reader, the present tense has sometimes been used to describe unfolding events.

threatened to break up" (Jonah 1:4). This wasn't some autumn breeze making the crew chilly; the ship was going to be smashed into pieces. What does Jonah do in the midst of this vicious storm? He takes a nap. Since it's not likely that he could have ignored the thrashing chaos all around him, he was probably terrified or shamed into a state of complete immobility, knowing the storm to be God's work. These are merely guesses, however, and we will never know the true reason. Whatever the cause, the rest of the crew finally springs into action, abandoning futile prayers to impotent gods and waking Jonah for assistance. They asked him which god he worshipped. Provoked into honest self-reflection, Jonah sees that there is no escape from his duty to God. Jonah can be an example to us all when he proclaims his faith without missing a beat: **"I am a Hebrew and I worship the LORD, the God of heaven, who made the sea and the land"** (Jonah 1:9). He walks up to the deck and calmly explains the situation to the rest of the crew. **"Pick me up and throw me into the sea,"** he replied, **"and it will become calm. I know that it is my fault that this great storm has come upon you"** (Jonah 1:12). Jonah is finally addressing his responsibilities, and even if it means encountering some other danger or even death, he's ready to face them head on.

Jonah is immediately swallowed up, not by a whale, as is commonly thought, but by a great fish. We remember this part of the story well because things like this never happen to us. But how can we be sure that God doesn't use powerful or dramatic intervention to get *us* to cooperate with His plan for *our* lives? Often we want to put difficult situations into our own context and timetable, when in reality we're working on God's timetable. I mentioned earlier that life was becoming increasingly difficult for me in my rebellion, and it wasn't until Christ called me to take my faith seriously that I began to see things more clearly. We must try to display patience and understanding when such things happen, as they are all part of God's plan. This is also true of the large-scale tragedies that are happening all around us, such as hurricanes, diseases, and terrorist attacks. Why do these things happen to us if God loves us? If we take time to examine these Biblical examples, we see that coddling isn't God's way. We are God's children, and as children we will not always understand the will of the Father. We despise the hardships which we know we deserve but never want to face nonetheless. These tragedies are the result of our sinful nature, and may God be glorified that He can create and strengthen faith in the midst of such adversity!

Children will almost always thank you in their own way for disciplining them fairly according to their conduct. Discipline may not always (if ever) turn into a situation where instant gratification takes effect, but often they *will* eventually thank you, and their lives *will* benefit from the discipline and love you have shown them. Jonah's words from the belly of the fish reveal his own budding understanding of the situation in which he finds himself. He says **"Those who cling to worthless idols forfeit the grace that could be theirs. But I, with a song of thanksgiving, will sacrifice to you. What I have vowed I will make good. Salvation comes from the LORD"** (Jonah 2:8-9). Now that Jonah has been shown the error of his ways, he is finally ready to take on the task which the Lord set before him in the opening chapter of the book. Jonah didn't make this decision out of fear, but because he was starting to accept that Nineveh must hear the Word of God in order to repent and be saved. Repentance is the foundation of a Christian's salvation. Without repentance, there can be no forgiveness of sins. It's vital that Jonah preach to these spiritually starved Ninevites!

So Jonah preaches God's Word – and what happens? THEY REPENT! Even the king **"rose from his throne, took off his royal robes, covered himself with sackcloth and sat down in the dust"** (Jonah 3:6). Wearing scratchy sackcloth and sitting in dirt or ashes were the traditional outward forms of repentance. So what brought these people to faith? Was it Jonah's awesome preaching style? This is doubtful since all that is mentioned of his preaching is that he did preach (**Jonah 3:4**). Throughout the Bible we find evidence of great things happening without a detailed explanation of why or how. We must simply credit these accomplishments to God. We should never focus our attention on *how* God does something, but simply on the fact that it has been done. I never imagined that transferring from a secular to a Christian university would change my view and life forever, but God thought otherwise. God's will is done, and we are given the choice to comply with it or to rebel, as many choose to their eventual downfall. We see this in the case of Jonah, who indeed fell but was picked back up.

Nineveh has repented and all is well for Jonah – or is it? God is pleased and Nineveh is faithful, but Jonah is furious. He wanted Nineveh, a city full of Israel's enemies, to burn to the ground! Just when you might fool yourself into thinking that Jonah's story is so legendary because of his extraordinary character, think again. Jonah's dismay – which was a mixture of jealousy at Nineveh's blind faith, anger at God's mercy, and damaged pride from being proven wrong – reveals his ordinary sinfulness. How does God deal with this cranky prophet? He comforts Jonah, who has been exposed to the penetrating heat of the desert sun, and tries to make life as easy for him as possible. **"Then the LORD God provided a vine and made it grow up over Jonah to give shade for his head to ease his discomfort, and Jonah was very happy about the vine"** (Jonah 4:6). We picture Jonah smiling to himself now, happy that the Lord has given him a reward for his hard work. But if the story had ended there, what would he have learned from all of this? Fortunately, God wasn't finished with Jonah yet. **"But at dawn the next day God provided a worm, which chewed the vine so that it**

withered. When the sun rose, God provided a scorching east wind, and the sun blazed on Jonah's head so that he grew faint" (Jonah 4:7-8).

Now things are just miserable for Jonah all over again. Is this what his hard work and obedience has earned him? We, too, often feel this way. We want to be rewarded in our own way and in our own time for what we've done. And how does Jonah, in a fit of depression, react? He says that he wants to die, as if that would be a proper solution to his mounting discomfort and misery. God even asks Jonah: **"Do you have a right to be angry about the vine?"** (Jonah 4:9). Of course, Jonah has no right to be angry, and God undoubtedly knows the answer to this rhetorical question. However, Jonah simply repeats his desire to stop living. Now God has sufficiently set the stage for a final lesson for Jonah, one which we can only assume gets through to him, since the book ends here. **"But the LORD said, 'You have been concerned about this vine, though you did not tend it or make it grow. It sprang up overnight and died overnight. But Nineveh has more than a hundred and twenty thousand people who cannot tell their right hand from their left, and many cattle as well. Should I not be concerned about that great city?'"** (Jonah 4:10-11). Here is a valuable lesson for us all. We want the Lord to fix every little bump in our road, and we are discouraged when He does not. We fail to realize that God *does* provide where it is needed. God doesn't bring these hardships into our lives (they are the result of sin), but He always provides the way out: **"No temptation has seized you except what is common to man. And God is faithful; he will not let you be tempted beyond what you can bear. But when you are tempted, he will also provide a way out so that you can stand up under it"** (1 Corinthians 10:13).

As our heavenly Father, God knows best which situations to make easy in our lives and which ones to let us struggle with, so that we can benefit and grow throughout the years. When His children are in a massive state of despair, such as the Ninevites, He finds a relatively "ordinary" means to get them to repent, namely Jonah. The wonderful message contained in the book of Jonah is that we are taken care of by our Lord. Oftentimes, however, the man behind the book is thrust into the spotlight. We can look up to Jonah as a hero of faith, and an example to all Christians, but we also need to keep God in focus. Without God working through his actions, Jonah would have hopped a ship out to the boonies of ancient civilization and taken the easy road. Just as with all ordinary people who make an incredible impact with the saving message of the Bible, Jonah needed the Lord's help to accomplish the extraordinary feat of Nineveh's repentance.

Study Questions

Q1. Right at the beginning of the book, we find Jonah running away from God (**1:3**). Why do you think he was so quick to run away? Do we ever run away from the responsibilities that God has placed into our lives? Why?

Q2. God sends Jonah a powerful message to get his attention (**1:4-5**). How did Jonah show that he understood that message? Who else witnessed God's power on that boat? Read **2 Corinthians 12:7-10**. What does Paul say about hardship?

Q3. If Jonah did, in fact, understand what God was telling Him, why did God send the fish to swallow him (**1:17**)? Read **Hebrews 12:3-11**. Does Jonah have more lessons to learn? God's actions certainly showed discipline. Did they also show grace?

Also read **Jonah 2** in its entirety. This prayer is a wonderful example of how we can go to God when in times of despair.

Q4. I make the comment on page 29 that repentance is the foundation of a Christian's salvation. Do you agree or disagree with that statement? How does repentance work? Is it something that comes from within us or is it something that God gives? Read **Romans 2:1-4**.

Q5. What is Jonah's reaction to Nineveh's repentance and belief (**4:1-3**)? Why does he respond this way? Does this make any sense to our way of thinking?

Q6. What are we supposed to learn from the vine narrative (**4:6-8**)? Is God picking on Jonah? Read **4:10-11**. Are we sometimes too inwardly focused to see the big picture?

Lydia

[14] One of those listening was a woman named Lydia, a dealer in purple cloth from the city of Thyatira, who was a worshiper of God. The Lord opened her heart to respond to Paul's message. [15] When she and the members of her household were baptized, she invited us to her home. "If you consider me a believer in the Lord," she said, "come and stay at my house." And she persuaded us. (Acts 16:14-15)

Casual readers of the Bible may not remember Lydia from their studies. However, although contained in only four verses of Scripture, Lydia's story of dynamic conversion is certainly worthy of closer examination. Someone better acquainted with the book of Acts may remember her as a "dealer of purple," but how is this relevant to us in our modern times? Purple dye was a product of the region of Philippi, where Lydia lived, making it quite valuable to travelers and visitors to the area, as well as for the locals who used it for their livelihood. We can assume from the text that Lydia was also a believer in the One True God[2]. We suppose this because she was present with the others who gathered to listen to Paul and Silas preach. In this largely pagan region, being both a business woman and a believer would have been a risky endeavor, especially the believing part.

---

[2] Faith in the One True God of Judaism reflects the active and living faith of characters of the Old Testament. In the Lydia chapter (which discusses events that take place after the incarnation of Jesus Christ), a distinction is made between faith in the One True God and faith in Jesus Christ.

Although Judaism was a recognized religion at this time, the mere fact that the women had to meet **"outside the city gate"** (Acts 16:13) leads one to believe that practicing Jews were few in number and not common in Philippi. Since Lydia (and we assume her entire family) depended on this trade in "purple goods," which were very expensive (Lydia's family apparently had great means), she had much to lose by listening to Paul. By reading the material directly following this narrative (**Acts 16:16-39**), we can see that Paul's message wasn't popular in this area, which was largely pagan. Professing belief, especially in Christ (as Lydia was about to do), had great consequences. She might have been treated like a second class citizen – both because of her belief *and* because she was a woman – hurting both her business and income. Whether or not this was the case, she *was* present to listen to the lesson of Paul as he preached in the area.

How does this fit into our own life experience? Have we ever put our faith on the back burner or covered it ever so slightly under the cloak of worldliness so we'd be more comfortable at work or in our other groups of interest? As previously noted, I used to be guilty of this "cloaking" as well. In fact, at times I would drink more and act worse than my friends so that I wouldn't be branded as a "goody-goody Christian." Showing my faith would have been social suicide, or so I thought. Perhaps Lydia was guilty of this thought process as well. We know that she went and listened to Paul; however, she still might not have readily displayed evidence of her faith in her place of business. This would have allowed all to see publicly that she was a follower of the One True God, and not a worshiper of the pagan idols so popular in her area. She could have lost her livelihood, her social circle, or even her family. The very fact that she was so successful in her business, as we will discover later, suggests that either she kept her faith under the rug or that

God allowed her to witness to others while still enjoying the bounty of His harvest. Either way, she wouldn't have been able to do anything apart from the gracious will of God, and more precisely Jesus Christ.

As Lydia listened to the preaching of Paul, she heard the wonderful message of Christ crucified, and we read that **"The Lord opened her heart to respond to Paul's message"** (Acts 16:14). This is how the Word of God works. We can read the Bible over and over, looking for proof that the truths contained within are real. We can listen to fervent Christians proclaiming "He is risen!" and telling us what that means for our salvation. However, until the Holy Spirit decides to work in our hearts, this message appears nothing more than a well spun folktale. The wonderful thing about our God is that He works in *us*; we don't work for *Him*. He is an active God, searching diligently and finding us even when we're doing our best to hide. More often than not He plucks us from the pit, clutching us to His bosom at the moment of our deepest despair. How great is the love of our God that He would seek out sinners! Just as in our own experiences with the Holy Spirit, Lydia is moved to action.

The very next thing that we read here is that **"she [Lydia] and the members of her household were baptized"** (Acts 16:15). Here's another lesson for us to observe. She feels the Holy Spirit working in her, and she's already a believer in the One True God, but she and Paul both see the need for baptism. Baptism is the spiritual regeneration of our bodies, where the Holy Spirit takes up residence in our hearts and the evil spirit of original sin is cast out. Paul, like any preacher worth his salt, has her baptized right away. Lydia's faith is evident in the fact that her entire household was baptized along with her. This means that her husband and children were baptized as well, even though they hadn't experienced the same amazing revelation upon hearing the Word. Baptism brings salvation and understanding, not the

other way around. We receive an indwelling of the Holy
Spirit when we are baptized, and we must take this precious
gift when it is offered to us. Lydia certainly understands the
magnitude of this gift, because she then offers a gift of her
own to the disciples.

**"'If you consider me a believer in the Lord,' she
said, 'come and stay at my house.' And she persuaded
us'"** (Acts 16:15). As disciples and travelers, the proposition
of comfortable lodging and hospitality would have been
enticing, but they still refuse her offer. This refusal may have
stemmed from a sense of obligation to continue spreading the
Gospel.   It might also have manifested from the Middle
Eastern tradition of politely refusing a first offer of hospitality
so as not to appear greedy.   Whatever the reason, Lydia
successfully persuades them, even challenging their faith in
her conversion. Here we truly see God working through this
ordinary person. Lydia has gone from being a profitable
merchant to housing the men of the Lord and easing their
burden.   Even today, laypeople in a congregation can do
similar things, such as volunteering for jobs around the
church and inviting the pastor and other church workers over
for meals. If you're ever in my parish, I hope you feel the
same way!

Now we really begin to see what wonders the Lord
has brought forth in Lydia's life. She has already shown
hospitality to the servants of God, but now she goes even
further in her service to the Lord. After a brief pause in her
story, we hear at the end of the chapter that **"After Paul and
Silas came out of the prison, they went to Lydia's house,
where they met with the brothers and encouraged them"**
(Acts 16:40).   It becomes fairly clear that Lydia has
established her home as a church where the growing numbers
of Christians were to meet and worship.   Ignoring all
potential consequences, including chastisement or bankruptcy, she devotes her home and life to God's work. Lydia

has truly experienced some major changes. She has transformed from a believing merchant, to a faithful Christian, to a pivotal missionary and church worker in her time! God worked in her life to show her a higher purpose, and we can still surmise that Lydia kept her business going. She could then generate funds for her new lifestyle and reach out to even more believers through her business dealings.

Many people mistakenly believe that because they are not employed as a pastor or other called church worker, they are not serving God through their career. The truth is that any vocation done for the glory of God, no matter how "ordinary," is equally pleasing in God's eyes. What an extraordinary concept! Whether you are working on Wall Street, pushing a broom, or preaching the Gospel, God appreciates your labors done in His name and sees you as His perfect child. Much like Lydia, we have the opportunity to live our lives for God, even if we are not professional church workers.

Study Questions

Q1. Lydia was the original "working mom." On pages 35-36, I speak of the risks involved in being both a believer and a business owner. What are these risks? Do we still have to deal with these today? Read **Matthew 10:22**. Is the life of a Christian easier than that of an unbeliever?

Q2. Lydia may have been a believer in the One True God (as many Gentiles were by this point), but she wasn't yet a Christian. What is so significant about the way that she came to faith? See page 37.

Q3. It's clear in this text that Lydia's faith came prior to her baptism. However, can we be certain that everyone in her family had faith before they were baptized (**verse 15**)?

Q4. Lydia and her family are now baptized Christians, and their lives will never be the same. How do we know this (**verse 15**)? Read **Luke 6:43-45** and **Philippians 2:13**. How are our lives completely changed when we become Christians?

Q5. Lydia turned her house into a meeting place for Christians after her conversion, as is evidenced by the return of Paul and Silas in **verse 40**. She was using what she had to help the apostles in their ministry. How do we faithfully serve God in our own vocations?

Elisha

¹⁹ Elijah went from there and found Elisha son of Shaphat. He was plowing with twelve yoke of oxen, and he himself was driving the twelfth pair. Elijah went up to him and threw his cloak around him. (1 Kings 19:19)

Elisha should not be confused with his famous predecessor, Elijah, although he appears destined for the same sort of career full of miracles and wonders. What's so comforting for the ordinary reader about Elisha's story is that while he's allowed to do amazing things, he credits the Lord for everything he is able to accomplish. Elisha's story begins with his life as a farmer – or more accurately, the son of a wealthy farmer from the region of Abel Meholah. One day while Elisha is out working the soil, Elijah, the great prophet of God, appears. We read that **"Elijah went up to him and threw his cloak around him"** (1 Kings 19:19). Right in the middle of an ordinary workday, Elisha finds himself Elijah's successor with absolutely no warning. This action clearly shows us that Elisha is simply a man and not some otherworldly presence. This is an important distinction to make, for what he accomplishes later (with the help of the Lord) would be enough to doubt his humanity!

I've noticed that the reality for most pastors who receive a call to professional ministry later in life is that they have to abandon an established livelihood in order to follow this new, and very strong, call. As with my life, I had to forego my plans for a professional communications career to serve in the pastoral ministry. My story is not nearly as extreme as some, however, and there are a few men attending the seminary who still drive luxury cars from a past life. Although they are now forced to live modestly and make large payments to the seminary, they understand this reality as God's will, and they accept the change. Even the non-professional church worker can approach Elisha's story with a sense of familiarity, because whenever one feels compelled to make a lifestyle change for the Lord, sacrifice and compromise become a part of life.

"So Elisha left him and went back. He took his yoke of oxen and slaughtered them. He burned the plowing equipment to cook the meat and gave it to the people, and they ate. Then he set out to follow Elijah and became his attendant" (1 Kings 19:21). Now there's no turning back! Just like the seminary student who sells his house and belongings so he can move his family across the country, or just like the businessman who elects to give his fortune to others, Elisha isn't even thinking about returning to his old life. Jesus reinforces this action in the book of Matthew when He proclaims **"Anyone who does not take his cross and follow me is not worthy of me"** (Matthew 10:38). Elisha, for one, has some incredible times ahead of him, and did well by not looking back. Change may bring hardship, but it also brings adventure – and, oftentimes, gratification. Similarly, when we place our trust in Christ, we know that we will always be provided for, no matter how difficult life may get – and it will be difficult at times. But God's promise for you is that He will care for you in this life until you should be called home to your final destination, heaven. There is no greater comfort.

Elisha, surprisingly, isn't mentioned again for several chapters after he leaves the family farm. The reader assumes that he is faithfully following Elijah as he performs the duties of his position as prophet and man of God. It is sufficient for us to understand that Elisha has witnessed many things in his apprenticeship, and it's almost time for him to assume his role as *the* prophet after Elijah. There are many prophets at this time, but Elisha will stand out above the rest.

Elisha's words – **"as surely as the LORD lives and as you live, I will not leave you [Elijah]"** (2 Kings 2:4) – assure us that he has become very close with his mentor, and their inevitable parting will be difficult for him. To reinforce the kind of man Elijah had become through God's grace, we see a small display of God's power working through him. The two prophets approach the Jordan, and instead of fording the river, Elijah **"took his cloak, rolled it up and struck the water with it. The water divided to the right and to the left, and the two of them crossed over on dry ground"** (2 Kings 2:8). In contrast to the similar event of Moses parting the Red Sea, Elijah's parting of the waters is a mere side thought. God has so empowered this man that such a minor miracle is an everyday occurrence! Elijah then asks his apprentice what he most desires before they part, and Elisha wisely asks him for a double portion of his spirit.

Instead of assuming that his spirit is his to grant, Elijah proclaims that if Elisha can see his departure to heaven, Elisha will receive his request. This places the act of the spiritual bestowing upon God and not Elijah, who only possessed such talents by the glory of God. Elisha's request also helps us to understand his mindset, and we can see that he already understands what his potential relationship with God will be. Just how do we know that Elisha is Elijah's real successor? The proof is in Elisha's very next action. Departing from that area, he parts the waters in exactly the same way that his teacher had done just a few verses earlier. There's a new prophet in town!

Now begins the time of Elisha and his wonderful and miraculous deeds. What makes Elisha particularly note-worthy (and a wonderful example for this book) is the particular way in which he approaches the many difficulties occurring so frequently in his life. Unlike natural human wisdom, which assumes that all power comes from within, he gives all credit to the Lord *from the beginning*. This outward expression of his faith is first made manifest in Jericho, which has been afflicted with unwholesome water that neither quenches thirst nor grows adequate crops. Elisha simply took some salt and **"went out to the spring and threw the salt into it, saying, 'This is what the LORD says: 'I have healed this water. Never again will it cause death or make the land unproductive.'' And the water has remained wholesome to this day"** (2 Kings 2:21-22).

Miracles like this etch themselves into our minds, and remain the stuff of legend thousands of years later. For Elisha, however, this is merely a warm-up. Here's the point to remember. Did Elisha have magic salt? Can a man do things like Elisha did? No, a man cannot and Elisha shouldn't be credited with supernatural powers. Nor did God favor Elisha more than He favors us, for we are all loved equally as God's children through the blood and merits of Jesus Christ. Once we get rid of this common misconception, we can really begin to enjoy reading about the miracles that God worked through Elisha and the equally wonderful salvation that we *all* receive in Christ!

Church workers (and more specifically pastors) are often treated with a level of respect and compassion that few others receive with such regularity. People admire the work that they do, and it shows in the kindness they offer to these servants of God. Sometimes, however, people don't respect the Gospel's message (Christ crucified for our sins), and they don't want to hear what its messengers have to say, either because it's contrary to their own wisdom or they are ashamed for fear of the law. This fear is worked in deep within the heart, accusing sinners of their inability to fulfill God's law – the inevitable consequence of which is terrifying. Although Elisha was loved and respected by many, he still met with his share of opposition. **"As he was walking along the road, some youths came out of the town [Bethel] and jeered at him. 'Go on up, you baldhead!' they said. 'Go**

on up, you baldhead!'" (2 Kings 2:23). The youth of Bethel needed to be taught a lesson in manners.

I won't go as far as to suggest that Elisha's next move could serve as a model for modern pastors, but I think it *does* provide for us a good example of what comes from getting in the way of the Lord's work. **"He [Elisha] turned around, looked at them and called down a curse on them in the name of the LORD. Then two bears came out of the woods and mauled forty-two of the youths"** (2 Kings 2:24). Again we see that Elisha has no super powers from within, but receives all he has from God. Certainly nobody wants to think about youth being mauled. But this story does highlight the importance of Elisha's ministry and man's inability to suppress the Word of God.

There are many wonderful books written about the Old Testament, with several of them speaking of each and every one of Elisha's works and deeds at great length, and with much more description. Our task, however, is simply to observe some of the major events in this man's life and see that he was indeed an "ordinary person" just like the rest of us, despite the miracles that God worked through him.

Elisha then goes to Shunem and is met by a faithful woman and her elderly husband, who care for the prophet for a time. He feels compelled to repay their kindness, and when he discovers that they are, regretfully, without child, states **"About this time next year you will hold a son in your arms"** (2 Kings 4:16), and it came to pass. This in itself is a miracle, one of Elisha's greatest, but there is more to come. Soon the woman's son became ill and died, and she was overcome with grief. After other methods failed, Elisha recognized his greatest tool and weapon – prayer. **"He went in, shut the door on the two of them and prayed to the LORD. Then he got on the bed and lay upon the boy, mouth to mouth, eyes to eyes, hands to hands. As he stretched himself out upon him, the boy's body grew**

warm. Elisha turned away and walked back and forth in the room and then got on the bed and stretched out upon him once more. The boy sneezed seven times and opened his eyes" (2 Kings 4:33-35). At first glance, the method behind this miracle seems random, but when you compare it to an earlier miracle by Elijah (**1 Kings 17:7-24**), you see that there's a direct correlation between the two events. The Lord, who has made these two men His prophets, is capable of all things, showing the reader that it doesn't matter if Elijah, Elisha, or Fred Smith is performing the miracle; the power is completely from the Lord!

Elisha's greatest known story is probably that of Naaman, commander of the army of the king of Aram. By all means he was a great and powerful man, but he suffered the worst affliction of his time – leprosy. Leprosy is nasty business. A person's body rots and falls to pieces. Lepers were sent into isolation, signaling all passers-by that they were leprous and were not to be touched or met face to face, because leprosy is very contagious. At this point you're probably saying to yourself: "All right, so he's going to cure this man's leprosy – big deal. It might be impressive if he hadn't already brought somebody back from the dead!" You would be justified in thinking this, but this miracle isn't only about the healing. It's also about the mission work involved.

The nations of Aram and Israel weren't exactly friends. When the king of Aram sends a request specifically for Elisha, who is a public figure in Israel, he is greatly humbling himself. It's notable that Naaman is drawn to God and directed to Elisha's healing prowess through the witness of a humble Israelite servant girl. Here, once again, God is working in the hearts of unbelievers through the witness and testimony of very ordinary folks. By God's grace, Naaman listens to her and asks his king for permission to go to this mighty man of God. The tension between the two kingdoms is made evident when the king of Israel receives the letter asking for help – and is outraged. He thinks that Aram is trying to start a war with him by asking the impossible. Elisha, upon hearing of the king's distress, simply says "bring Naaman to me." Elisha's instructions for Naaman were simple: **"Go, wash yourself seven times in the Jordan, and your flesh will be restored and you will be cleansed"** (2 Kings 5:10).

This appears to be a simple request, and Naaman should have been overjoyed to hear that his healing would be so easy, but he wasn't. Just like people who reject the clear message of forgiveness in Jesus Christ, Naaman felt that Elisha's instructions were just too good to be true. We picture him drooping in his saddle upon the journey home, thumbing his nose at the dirty old Jordan River. Eventually, however, Naaman's discomfort – and a gentle nudge from his subordinates – led him to follow Elisha's advice. His healing was so thorough that **"his flesh was restored and became clean like that of a young boy"** (2 Kings 5:14). Now that he's healed, the real power behind this story shines through.

Naaman went right back to Elisha and said **"Now I know that there is no God in all the world except in Israel. Please accept now a gift from your servant"** (2 Kings 5:15). Elisha, acting as God's representative, would not accept Naaman's treasures. God's love is not subject to our actions and He's not interested in our worldly gifts, only our faith and love. Picture a modern day general of a heathen army. The general has a great deal of influence over his soldiers, and a respected leader like Naaman would almost serve as a father to his subordinates. Now that he's confessed his faith in the One True God, he will certainly share that faith with his people.

The truly miraculous power of God's love isn't fully revealed in the healings and resurrections that we see in these narratives. The greatest result of Elisha's interaction with Naaman is that he will now share his faith with everyone he meets, and many more souls will come to believe in the One True God of Israel, and ultimately in Jesus Christ Himself. From an ex-farmer to a lowly servant girl and even a heathen General...the story of Elisha proves that anyone, no matter how ordinary, can be a true servant of God's extraordinary Word!

Study Questions

Q1. In **1 Kings 19:19**, Elijah picks Elisha as his successor. What is significant about this? Why pick a successor at all? Is this something that we see today as well?

Q2. God selects many prophets to carry out His work. We usually think of such men as Elijah, Elisha, Isaiah, Jeremiah, and many others. Read **Deuteronomy 18:15-18**. What was the purpose of these prophets? Read **Hebrews 3:1-6**. How can we say that Jesus is the last prophet? What is Jesus saying in **Matthew 5:17**?

Q3. Change is hard, especially when we are set in our ways. It's hard to break out of our comfort zone unless we have to. See pages 43-44. How can Elisha's willingness to adapt serve as an example to us when change is necessary in our own lives?

Q4. God allowed Elisha to perform some pretty amazing feats. He parts a river (**2 Kings 2:8**), purifies a polluted water source with salt (**2 Kings 2:21-22**), predicts a barren woman's pregnancy (**2 Kings 4:16**), and even raises the dead (**2 Kings 4:34-35**). Some of these are performed with his cloak or some salt, but what is the greatest tool in his arsenal? See **2 Kings 4:33** and also **Mark 9:28-29**.

Q5. God works great and miraculous things even through the most humble (and ordinary) of His people. How is this proven in the account of Naaman? See page 48 and also **2 Kings 5:2-3**. What does this account teach us about the nature of Christian witness?

Q6. At first Naaman refuses to be cleansed. Why? See **2 Kings 5:10-12**. How is this similar to modern refusal of God's gifts in Baptism and the Lord's Supper?

Esther

¹⁷ The king was attracted to Esther more than to any of the other women, and she won his favor and approval more than any of the other virgins. So he set a royal crown on her head and made her queen. (Esther 2:17)

We've all seen those children's movies in which a young peasant girl with no chance for the throne falls in love with a prince (and vice versa) and eventually becomes queen, supposedly living "happily ever after." Disney has created an empire with many such movies, and they do entertain us with the idea of such fantasy happening in our own lives. As we grow older, however, we often begin to see them as silly and contrived. They just don't fit the pattern of our own lives – or do they? Whether or not the Hollywood film makers are aware of it, this scenario has already happened to a real girl – Esther! You know by now that people in the Bible don't necessarily follow a smooth pattern to their eventual greatness. The hypothetical quilt of Biblical greatness appears to be a patchworked mess except for one common thread – all great characters in the Bible trust in the Lord. These stories are living proof that God provides in every situation. The variety we see in such examples serves as evidence that God will provide even in our own lives, which are as diverse as grains of sand on a shore or stars in the sky.

It's been said that if you put your trust in the Lord, everything will be provided. I've heard simply amazing stories from seminarians and other believers regarding their reception of financial assistance just when they needed it most. For instance, I've heard of guys at the seminary getting laptops at the precise moment of their greatest need. I myself have received thousands of dollars here and there, seemingly out of the blue, when I needed just that much money for my seminary tuition. God's gifts aren't limited to the financial, either, and we see examples of His love every day as we live healthy, productive lives. If God is so good and gracious to the people of the Bible, just think of the wonders that He will work within your life as well! Esther's story is quite extreme, and she certainly enjoys a material life that we will never know, but the amazing reality is that God loves you and I every bit as much as He loves Esther! He shows this to us every day in the blessings that He provides for us, both large and small.

To understand how Esther was even given the opportunity to become queen, the stage must be properly set. King Xerxes had a large feast, and there was much to drink. When he had his fill of wine, he summoned his wife, Vashti, to come out **"wearing her royal crown, in order to display her beauty to the people and nobles, for she was lovely to look at"** (Esther 1:11). We don't know what else she was supposed to wear besides her crown (perhaps nothing), but she turned his request down flatly. Modern women might (and probably should) applaud Vashti for her boldness and pride, but these actions weren't as respected in her culture and age. She was ejected from her spot as queen and ordered never to see Xerxes again. The stage was officially set for a replacement to take the throne alongside the king. Oh, and one more thing: Xerxes then, in his infinite wisdom (note the sarcasm), issued a decree to the surrounding areas for men to enforce their authority over their wives, lest women believe that it's permissible to disobey a direct order from a man. At this point one might wonder why any woman would want to be married to such a tyrant.

Fortunately for Esther, the only condition for a woman to apply to be the king's bride was that she be beautiful and a virgin. Esther was both of these, so she was qualified to try. However, she was also an orphan, raised by her cousin Mordecai, and she was a Jew, which would likely hurt her chances for being selected. With so many natural barriers between her and the throne, how could poor Esther ever become queen? Fortunately, Esther was not only beautiful, but also very cunning and wise. We read that one way or another, she **"pleased him [Hegai, the eunuch in charge of this competition] and won his favor. Immediately he provided her with her beauty treatments and special food. He assigned to her seven maids selected from the king's palace and moved her and her maids into the best place in the harem"** (Esther 2:9).

Hegai, being a Eunuch, certainly sought no sexual reward from Esther for this special treatment, but her beauty and charm won him over so much that she was immediately the forerunner. It's also notable that she **"had not revealed her nationality and family background, because Mordecai had forbidden her to do so"** (Esther 2:10). This was a smart girl from a smart family. Even if she hadn't been the most beautiful girl (which she was), she was the brightest – at least with the guidance of Mordecai. But she was also very ordinary, wasn't she? Esther had about as much chance to become Xerxes' queen as she would to become the President of the United States. By all means the odds were against her (in race, gender, and social status), but with God nothing is impossible. God had great plans for her, and she followed them right to the throne, where she could really make a difference. But how did she get there?

The virgins were now to ask for whatever they wanted to take to the palace. When they arrived there, they each spent the night and returned the next morning. If the king was pleased with this part of the competition, his favorite virgins would get a call back. It's almost as tense as a reality television show, waiting to see who the king would select as his queen of choice. Fortunately, we also know that he'll soon make the right decision. Esther didn't go into this competition lightly, and she did everything just as Hegai had instructed her. **"Now the king was attracted to Esther more than to any of the other women, and she won his favor and approval more than any of the other virgins. So he set a royal crown on her head and made her queen instead of Vashti"** (Esther 2:17). Now Esther is queen and no longer an estranged Jew fighting for survival. However, God's extraordinary work through this ordinary woman had just begun.

Esther's first opportunity to test her newfound power reveals itself immediately. A man named Haman eventually found favor with the king, who in turn made him the second most powerful man in the kingdom. Soon Haman was commanding the others to bow to him and give him the proper respect. When Haman confronts Mordecai, however, he finds that the man will not bow to him. Those who know their Bible quite well have heard this sort of thing before. Faithful Jews will often refuse to bow to men, but instead only to God, and God in turn never lets them down. Haman, not interested in Jewish custom or beliefs, decides that Mordecai should die for his insubordination. Angered into blind fury, and desiring the most savage retribution for his freshly wounded pride, he resolves that all Jews should die.

In order to put this new resolution into action, the king himself would have to agree to such capital punishment. So Haman went to Xerxes with his plan. **"There is a certain people dispersed and scattered among the peoples in all the provinces of your kingdom whose customs are different from those of all other people and who do not obey the king's laws; it is not in the king's best interest to tolerate them. If it pleases the king, let a decree be issued to destroy them, and I will put ten thousand talents of silver into the royal treasury for the men who carry out this business"** (Esther 3:8-9). It is clear that Haman is serious about his plan, and with roughly 375 tons of silver allocated to the men who kill them, many are going to be eager to fulfill this wicked deed. Again, God's chosen people find themselves in a bind – with a tremendous price on their heads – but we know that the Lord will come to their aid.

After mourning for his life and the lives of his people, Mordecai decides to talk to Esther about this difficult situation and ask if she will make an appeal to the king. Esther tells him that anyone who goes to the king uninvited will be put to death, including the queen – and she hasn't been invited for a month. Mordecai wisely reminds her that if she doesn't use her position of authority to help her people, her fate will be the same as Xerxes' when the Lord strikes back. In other words, the consequences of her actions will be eternal. Esther is at a difficult crossroads. What should she do? In the end, she makes the right decision – not the one that grants her glory on this earth, but the one that keeps her faithful to the Lord. Even within the palace walls, she can remember that all of this material wealth that surrounds her was given to her by God. She must be willing to sacrifice it for the good of His people. Many of us today would have a very difficult time giving up a comfortable lifestyle in order to help out those in need, and most of the time we don't. Dependence on wealth and material goods is a huge stumbling block for Christians and non-Christians alike. This is the kind of thing that Jesus was talking about when He said **"it is easier for a camel to go through the eye of a needle than for a rich man to enter the kingdom of God"** (Matthew 19:24). This statement has nothing to do with camels or needles. It means that when we amass wealth we are often tempted to depend on that wealth instead of on the awesome power of God. Instead, with eyes of faith firmly placed upon Jesus Christ, we can expect everything we need in this life and the next!

So what does Esther do next? She approaches the king, unannounced, and he's actually pleased to see her (thank God)!   He pardons her life and even offers her anything she wants – even up to half of his kingdom! This is even more temptation and pressure for Esther to give up her cause and take the easy road, but she doesn't. She cleverly asks that he and Haman join her for a banquet that she'll prepare. At that time, she'll tell him what she wants. Instead of just blurting out her request and risking a refusal, she entices the king to play along with her.

Xerxes comes to the banquet, drinks his fill, and again offers her almost anything her heart desires. Esther smartly detains him once more with the same request for a banquet in which he and Haman are the guests of honor. Why Haman, you might ask yourself.   Rest assured that Esther's plan becomes very clear soon enough. They meet a third time – king, queen, and honored guest – when Esther finally asks her favor. **"If I have found favor with you, O king, and if it pleases your majesty, grant me my life – this is my petition. And spare my people – this is my request. For I and my people have been sold for destruction and slaughter and annihilation. If we had merely been sold as male and female slaves, I would have kept quiet, because no such distress would justify disturbing the king"** (Esther 7:3-4). What a clever woman! She tells the king something that would absolutely horrify him, reminds him that he's too important to listen to any lesser pleas, and sounds so darn innocent! By this time, you can just bet that Xerxes is ready to hang the traitor that came up with this sickening idea of killing the Jews, his beloved wife's own people! Esther points her finger at Haman, who is subsequently hanged, and her people are saved.

What about poor old Mordecai? Doesn't he benefit from all his hard work and faithfulness in this tale? Yes, he does! Mordecai, who'd already been recognized once for his services to the king, is given Haman's position, which makes him second in command over the entire kingdom. Xerxes even allows him to write an edict to his people, giving them the right to defend themselves against the enemy. The king couldn't change the first edict, which ordered an attack, but he could give the Jews every fair advantage. Mordecai grew in power and prestige until he was **"preeminent among the Jews, and held in high esteem by his many fellow Jews, because he worked for the good of his people and spoke up for the welfare of all the Jews"** (Esther 10:3). With Mordecai as Xerxes' second in command, God's chosen people could expect many years of peace and cooperation with the more powerful Persian nation. God had truly blessed His children through the work of Queen Esther!

Esther's tale shows us that with God, nothing ordinary stays ordinary. Not all of us will attain a kingdom here on earth by the hand of the Lord, but we can look forward to receiving something much greater. Our eternal and heavenly kingdom has been won for us by Jesus Christ and His atoning sacrifice on the cross. When we die and leave behind this temporal life, we'll be reunited with Esther and all the rest of the faithful who have helped to keep the name of the Lord prominent among the heathen.

Study Questions

Q1. I speak of a common thread in the quilt of Biblical greatness on page 53. What is this thread? Read **Romans 10:11-13**. What can we expect if we follow in this "thread of greatness?"

Q2. Esther was certainly ordinary, although she had vast intrinsic gifts at her disposal. See pages 54-55. What were some of these gifts? Read **Matthew 25:14-30**. What is significant about the way Esther uses her gifts (talents)?

Q3. Read **Esther 3:1-6**. Mordecai makes a bold move in refusing to bow to his earthly superior, Haman. As a Jew, he was to bow to God alone (**Exodus 20:2-6**). We see examples of this also in **Daniel 3:12-19** and **6:13**. How do we as Christians continue this tradition even today? Or, perhaps, how do we fail to carry this on? Read **Romans 13:1-7**.

Q4. After Mordecai's refusal to bow to Haman, the Jews find themselves in a terrible bind (**Esther 3:8-9**). Read **Esther 4:12-14**, where Mordecai reminds Esther of her obligation to her people and her God. Esther must choose between her position of earthly power and her beliefs. Do we ever find ourselves in such a position? How does Esther respond (**Esther 4:15-16**)?

Q5. Esther, aside from being a fair and gracious queen, is a terrific Biblical model for wives even today. This may surprise you in light of her husband's atrocious behavior (**Esther 1:10-12, 22**). However, bad behavior on the part of one spouse shouldn't correlate to both sides of the relationship. Read **Esther 4:10-16, 5:1-8, 7:1-4**. How was Esther a good wife? See also **Ephesians 5:22-33**.

Ruth

[16] Ruth replied, "Don't urge me to leave you or to turn back from you. Where you go I will go, and where you stay I will stay. Your people will be my people and your God my God." (Ruth 1:16)

Just when you may have thought that only great and miraculous events in the Bible are worthy of mention, along comes Ruth. Most of us know that there's a book in the Bible called Ruth, and that it's really quite short (only four chapters). If you can't remember what Ruth actually does, that's because she might not appear to do much at all. In reality, Ruth does exactly what she needs to, integrating smoothly within that common thread of belief that we've been discussing. Her lack of amazing tales only exemplifies God's great power in her life. Ruth is our cover girl, and we hold her in high esteem as one of the ordinary. She performs no miracles or healings, and she doesn't bring anyone back to life. Ruth doesn't boldly sacrifice her own safety for that of her people – as Esther has done – nor does she find herself in any position of authority. This story intentionally keeps Ruth away from the miraculous, which tells us that while Ruth was an essential part of Biblical history, she didn't really do anything exceptional on her own. It was all from God.

Some business models render their employees nothing more than cogs in a wheel, saying that every part needs to be working just right for the machine of industry to keep moving forward. While the Bible certainly doesn't break its characters into such metaphorical simplicities, Ruth is essentially a cog in the great wheel of the Bible narrative, not to mention Earth's history. If she had failed to do what God allowed her to do, all would have been lost. For her success, and for carrying her every step of the way, we thank God. So what exactly is Ruth's story?

The book of Ruth begins with a man named Elimelech, with Ruth herself just a side note. You're probably wondering who Elimelech is, and you're not alone. He plays a very small role in this very short book. Without Elimelech and his family ties, however, Ruth wouldn't have done what she did. This makes him an essential part of Biblical history. Ruth's story begins when she marries into this growing family. Elimelech marries Naomi, they have two boys, and the boys marry girls from other areas. Before Ruth's part of the story really gets going, we witness not only the death of Elimelech (we don't know how or why), but also of his boys, leaving only Naomi with her two daughters-in-law: Orpah and Ruth.

This isn't modern times, and for three women to make any kind of living, they were compelled by necessity to remarry. Before they could worry about that, however, they have to survive the famine. **"When she heard in Moab that the LORD had come to the aid of his people by providing food for them, Naomi and her daughters-in-law prepared to return home from there. With her two daughters-in-law she left the place where she'd been living and set out on the road that would take them back to the land of Judah"** (Ruth 1:6-7). In order to stay alive, the women decide to travel to Bethlehem in Judah, the land of Naomi's people. The distance from Moab to Bethlehem is about 100 miles, and they had to travel by foot! What would take us less than two hours of driving on the interstate would involve several days of arduous and potentially life-threatening travel for Naomi and her daughters-in-law.

Once they arrive, the real story of Ruth begins to take place. Safely in Bethlehem, Naomi instructs the young women to go home in search of new husbands. When they shrug off her desperate pleas to seek a new life, she insists.

"Why would you come with me? Am I going to have any more sons, who could become your husbands? Return home, my daughters; I am too old to have another husband. Even if I thought there was still hope for me – even if I had a husband tonight and then gave birth to sons – would you wait until they grew up? Would you remain unmarried for them?" (Ruth 1:11-13).

Naomi's reasoning is rock solid. She's now a widow, sitting at the bottom of the social ladder and facing a very difficult and meager existence. These girls are still in their prime, able to marry other men and have good lives. She even tells them that there's no chance for marriage at all if they stay with her. Unless they want to live the life of a widow at this young age, they must go their own ways. While it's significant that both girls argue to stay, Orpah departs after Naomi's speech. Ruth, however, literally clings to her mother-in-law, making one of the greatest statements of faith in the Bible. **"Where you go I will go, and where you stay I will stay. Your people will be my people and your God my God. Where you die I will die, and there I will be buried. May the LORD deal with me, be it ever so severely, if anything but death separates you and me"** (Ruth 1:16-17).

What reason could there possibly be to stay with Naomi? Note Ruth's statement that "your God will be my God." Here is the crux of the issue. Moab is a nation of pagans who sacrificed and worshiped to bronze statues and other "dead items." Bethlehem, the land of Naomi and Elimelech, is a nation of believers. God has not given Ruth the power to heal the sick or raise the dead, but she believes in Him with all of her heart. She is more than willing to give up a potentially comfortable life to serve Him. This is pleasing to God, and this is what makes Ruth a true hero of faith. Maybe you know men and women like this, who choose occupations such as social work, Christian school teaching, volunteering, or even shepherding God's flock as a pastor, all of which seldom reap great material rewards in this life. Of course, the Lord is honored through any vocation when the work is done for His glory. Ruth here understands that the rewards for her in heaven are much greater than anything she might receive on earth, so she takes a leap of faith.

One chapter of Ruth's life closes as another opens. There may be a chance for Ruth to enjoy some comfort and pleasure in this life as well. God doesn't want us to suffer and be miserable all of the time. Quite the opposite! God is the reason for every good thing in our lives. The cross of Christ offers us both eternal life and the assurance that God will provide the smaller, temporal things that we enjoy every day, such as our homes, cars, and food on the table. Ruth isn't putting her hope in these material things. However, she can still receive them without any feelings of guilt, because she sees all blessings in her life as a gift from God. What is Ruth's temporal gift? A man named Boaz.

Boaz is Elimelech's relative, and as such he must offer a small bit of kindness to Naomi and Ruth (Elimelech's widow and daughter-in-law, respectively). Ruth is working his fields, taking a small amount of the grain for her and Naomi, when she's spotted by Boaz, who doesn't know her at all. He asks about her and finds out that she's family, which is all he needs to hear. He approaches Ruth and welcomes her. **"My daughter, listen to me. Don't go and glean in another field and don't go away from here. Stay here with my servant girls. Watch the field where the men are harvesting, and follow along after the girls. I have told the men not to touch you. And whenever you are thirsty, go and get a drink from the water jars the men have filled"** (Ruth 2:8-9). Boaz is showing himself to be a good and honorable man, and for several reasons.

First of all, Ruth doesn't need to be scrounging around for wheat all day, even though that would have been kind enough of Boaz. As the previous Bible reference points out, Boaz has offered her the choice bounty of his harvest under the protection of his watchful eye. Perhaps a lesser man would have been content to let her fend for herself, but Boaz is a believer, as becomes apparent through his actions. We also see that Boaz is one of the first advocates of the sexual harassment code of ethics. In those days men could have treated Ruth in whatever manner they wished. As a widow with no male protection, she would have been at the bottom of the social ladder, susceptible to any advances they might make. Boaz, however, has warned them that such actions will feel the brunt of his anger. Women in his care are to be treated with respect, and he is certainly going above and beyond the call of duty with such commands. He then explains why he has been so kind to her. **"I've been told all about what you have done for your mother-in-law since the death of your husband – how you left your father and mother and your homeland and came to live with a people you did not know before. May the LORD repay you for what you have done. May you be richly rewarded by the LORD, the God of Israel, under whose wings you have come to take refuge"** (Ruth 2:11-12). Boaz made it clear that this was the will of the Lord, and that Ruth was now living under His grace, not because she had stayed with her mother-in-law (although this certainly impressed Boaz), but because she had chosen – against all odds – to follow the One True God.

Have you ever made a decision like Ruth's? Have you ever made a leap of faith, regardless of the consequence? My decision to enter the seminary was certainly such a leap. I hadn't really read the Bible very much and I knew even less of church doctrine when I entered the seminary. By all means, I shouldn't have been let in the front doors, but the

Lord willed otherwise. He was gently guiding me through my decisions to serve Him. I look forward to a fruitful ministry because the Lord guides my steps. We don't always feel the Lord nudging us along, but when you make a decision that reaps amazing benefits or brings you closer to Christ, you can bet that the Holy Spirit was hard at work in your life. Boaz wanted Ruth to realize this, making his point very clear not only in his words, but also through his actions.

Eventually Ruth winds up at home with an immense amount of grain. Naomi, who was a very bright woman, was pleasantly surprised by Boaz's kindness, and immediately hatched up a plan. What seemed to Ruth to be a way to stay alive and enjoy the kindness of a relative was much more to Naomi. **"Wash and perfume yourself, and put on your best clothes. Then go down to the threshing floor, but don't let him [Boaz] know you are there until he has finished eating and drinking. When he lies down, note the place where he is lying. Then go and uncover his feet and lie down. He will tell you what to do"** (Ruth 3:3-4). Nothing about this plan seems sexual. This isn't a scheme to excite the lusts of Boaz, or to make him do something indecent so that Naomi and Ruth can blackmail him for more generosity. Ruth's asking him to marry her, but much more than that, she's asking him to become her kinsman-redeemer.

So what exactly is a kinsman-redeemer? If Boaz agrees to this, he'll be responsible for Ruth, her deceased husband's property, and Naomi and Elimelech's property. As their kinsman-redeemer, he'll basically be receiving the whole group under his roof and taking care of them. Boaz is a good and honorable man, but what are his limits? This seems almost too much for one person to handle, but God will accomplish His work. Boaz was placed in Ruth's life for a purpose, which we'll discover shortly. In our own lives, God works through a variety of people to shape us into who we are and what we will be. In the first part of the book, I wrote about my wife Andrea and how much she had done for me. Even if she had married someone else, the changes and improvements that she brought out in me through her love, prayer, and devotion were permanent, and I still would have entered the ministry. However, as my wife, she'll continue to strengthen my ministry and my devotion to Christ for the rest of our lives. I can never repay her for this. God put her in my life for a reason and vice versa. God put Boaz in Ruth's life for a reason and vice versa. If Boaz should accept Ruth, he'll see what benefits the Lord has in store for him.

Boaz, the picture of honor, instructs Ruth to stay the night so as to avoid being seen as a harlot, but he doesn't touch her. Instead, he explains that he is overjoyed to take this very difficult and committed position in her life, but he is not entitled to it. There is one closer in relation than he and he must make sure that this man doesn't want to take the offer first. God is showing us here that the union of Boaz and Ruth is totally pure and without trickery. Boaz is going to great lengths to make his marriage to Ruth legitimate. So how do these legal proceedings go?

The other man, the would-be kinsman-redeemer, seems happy to take Ruth as his wife, but there's more to this agreement than that. Boaz explains: **"'On the day you buy the land from Naomi and from Ruth the Moabitess, you acquire the dead man's widow, in order to maintain the name of the dead with his property.' At this, the kinsman-redeemer said, 'Then I cannot redeem it because I might endanger my own estate. You redeem it yourself. I cannot do it'"** (Ruth 4:5-6). Note the contrast between the selfish mindset of this new man and the kind, benevolent attitude of Boaz. The would-be kinsman-redeemer doesn't want to receive this extra burden in his life, so he refuses, giving Boaz the right to take it all upon himself. What the other man didn't realize were the glorious events that would surround this union.

Ruth and Boaz lived happily ever after (as much as anyone can expect) as husband and wife, but their story at this point is less significant than their child, Obed. Obed's genealogy follows the account of his birth. **"He was the father of Jesse, the father of David"** (Ruth 4:17). Ruth's child, a main reason for her existence, is the grandfather of King David, who would later be considered the greatest king that ever ruled Israel. David, one of the greatest figures in all of Biblical literature, owes his existence to God's gracious will and an ordinary woman from Moab who wouldn't give up on her family. David would have numerous descendants, the most worthy of mention certainly being Jesus the Christ. This descendent of Ruth would go on to save the world from its sins. The same Christ that saves you and me is also Ruth's Savior. Jesus is *our* kinsman-redeemer, taking all of our burdens upon Himself, paying the debt for (redeeming) our sin, and freeing us to live joyfully as God's children! We must never think that our efforts for the Lord are small and insignificant. We may be ordinary, but our efforts are all part of His glorious plan. Whether or not we see the benefits in our lifetime, they'll ultimately serve His will in the highest possible way.

Study Questions

Q1. Ruth appears very ordinary at first. In reality, she is anything *but* ordinary because she yielded to God's guiding hand. Have you known people in your own life who appear quite unexceptional, only to find God is accomplishing great things through them?

Q2. See page 64. Ruth's life at first appears to be filled with difficulties and hardship. Her husband dies and she is forced – with her widowed mother-in-law and sister-in-law – to leave her home of Moab for the foreign land of Judah. All she has to look forward to is a hundred mile trek across barren lands in search of food and support. Do our lives ever appear hopeless with nothing to look forward to? Is there any happiness to be found in suffering? Read **Romans 5:1-5** and also **1 Peter 1:6-7**.

Q3. Read **Ruth 1:11-13**. Naomi gives her daughters-in-law a justifiable excuse to leave her once they arrive safely at Judah. Ruth and Orpah, although not from this land, could go back to their old lifestyle, marry well, and live in relative comfort. Staying with Naomi would mean certain poverty and hardship, since Naomi's family was under no obligation to care for her or a daughter-in-law who was of age to be remarried. Read **Ruth 1:14-17**. What do the girls do? What would you do in this situation?

Q4. See page 66. Ruth is richly blessed by God for her obedience. Her blessing comes in the form of a man named Boaz. Read **Ruth 2:1-23**. Who is Boaz (**2:1**)? How has he come to enter her life (**2:3**)? What sort of man is he?

Q5. When Naomi hears of Boaz's great kindness to Ruth, she devises a plan (**3:3-4**). What was her plan? What is the result (**3:6-13**)? How do we know that God's favor was with Ruth and Naomi?

Q6. Although Boaz accepts the role of kinsman-redeemer for Ruth and Naomi, he is not the next in line to claim such a position. What must be done before Boaz can accept Ruth's offer (**3:12-13**)? What is the result of this (**4:5-6**)? Do you have a kinsman-redeemer? Do you need one? Read **Galatians 3:10-14**, **Titus 2:11-14**, and **1 Peter 1:18-19**.

Q7. Ruth's greatest contribution to humanity came long after her death. Who was the great-grandson of Ruth and Boaz (**4:17**)? What does this say about our own lives?

Nicodemus

¹ Now there was a man of the Pharisees named Nicodemus, a member of the Jewish ruling council. ² He came to Jesus at night and said, "Rabbi, we know you are a teacher who has come from God. For no one could perform the miraculous signs you are doing if God were not with him." (John 3:1-2)

Nicodemus is one of those Biblical characters that you'll miss if you should happen to blink during your study. He's mentioned in three chapters in only one book in the New Testament. When the Gospel writers want something to really stand out, they include it more than once. Nicodemus is included only in John's Gospel, and briefly at that. In our studies, we have been taking a careful second look at those characters who usually don't receive a lot of attention. Deep within these minor Biblical players are lessons and virtues which we can – and should – embody in our own lives. Nicodemus is someone whom we may easily identify with, because he's quite human. In fact, he's pretty dense. Isn't that just like you and me? He actually gets to talk with Jesus face to face and he doesn't add anything to the conversation. Upon further study, you may see yourself as a Nicodemus. If this should happen, don't be alarmed. There's a bit of Nicodemus in all of us.

The book of John starts with a bang, and doesn't slow down. We're immediately challenged by the fact that Jesus Christ is the creator of the entire world, and that He is the one who formed each and every one of us. Then we are presented with John the Baptist, whose calling it is to prepare the way for the coming Messiah. John doesn't portray a warm and fuzzy birth narrative for Christ, such as those you may hear in church on Christmas Eve. No, the Jesus of John's narrative is the mighty Creator and Redeemer of the world, and He begins His work immediately. Two major things happen in the life of our Savior before the account of Nicodemus even takes place. First, Jesus has already turned the water at the wedding in Cana into wine, which is one of His best known miracles. Secondly, He has also cleared the temple of merchants and vagrants, which showcases Jesus' passion and sense of urgent duty among the people of Israel. In the midst of all of this action, a man quietly approaches Jesus. This is an ordinary, unassuming man, and he comes to Jesus under cover of darkness. You can almost feel the silence of night closing in around these two as they converse – just a man and his Savior.

Nicodemus begins the conversation in ignorance, and we can see right away that he doesn't understand the full gravity of the situation. **"Rabbi, we know you are a teacher who has come from God. For no one could perform the miraculous signs you are doing if God were not with him"** (John 3:2). With this comment, Nicodemus is already showing himself to be a different kind of Pharisee. As the spiritual leaders of the Jews, most Pharisees felt threatened by Jesus' ministry and sought to discredit Him. He often pointed out their abuse of power and claimed that God's love was for the Gentiles as well as the Jews, which was heresy to their way of thinking. Conversely, Nicodemus sees Jesus as someone special, and is convinced that God's hand is with this man and His ministry. Jesus, however, being the Great Teacher, challenges what Nicodemus *thinks* he knows with His first comment. **"I tell you the truth, no one can see the kingdom of God unless he is born again"** (John 3:3). Huh? How is this a reply to what Nicodemus first said?

Nicodemus has every right to be flustered by this Man's apparent attempt to skirt around the real issue. From this incident we begin to realize the danger of reading the

Bible without the influence of the Holy Spirit. Without help, one cannot truly interpret these passages, much as Nicodemus cannot interpret the words of the Lord. In the Lutheran Church, we use such tools as Luther's Catechism, which is a concise review of all that is necessary for salvation, taken directly from the Bible. If one can understand what is written in the Catechism, then that person is one step closer to knowing the overall message of salvation in the Bible. Other Christian denominations also use similar materials. It's not wise to assume that you can understand the wisdom of the Bible without a little foreknowledge. Nicodemus, being an ordinary guy, had no catechism knowledge, and he wears his ignorance on his sleeve.

    "'How can a man be born when he is old?' Nicodemus asked. 'Surely he cannot enter a second time into his mother's womb to be born!'" (John 3:4). If he had even the slightest understanding of Jesus and His ministry, this foolish man wouldn't have misinterpreted the words of our Lord. As it were, he makes a rather silly and incoherent comment about what is possible and what is not possible with God. The word that Jesus used here in the text, which has been translated "born again," also means "born from above." If Nicodemus had realized this, he might have known that this is a different kind of birth from the first one he had as a baby. This is the birth experienced in the waters of baptism. Since I've already described baptism, I won't elaborate on its necessity again here beyond mentioning that we actually die with Christ in our baptism and are raised to new life through the water and Word. So far, Nicodemus seems more like an inhibitor of faith than a hero, but that's what makes these Biblical heroes so special. God makes great things happen through them *despite* their shortcomings.

    Your pastor does his best to share the Word of God with you and make it understandable and applicable to your life. Other Christians strive to do the same. However, all human beings are unworthy of such a task and fall short of it every day. Through the witness of your pastor or another Christian, you may come to know the message of the Bible as your own and devote your life to Christ. This is wonderful and surely the goal of any ministry. However, realize that it was not the mediocre efforts of a Christian witness that saved you, but the Holy Spirit working *through* him or her. This is why we must never hold back from spreading the message of Jesus Christ because we feel unworthy. No human is worthy of such a task. The success that we experience as Christians in our witness stems not from ourselves, but from the Holy Spirit. So what kind of birth is Christ talking about? We want to apply human reason to this statement and say that Christ wants us to start living our lives like dedicated Christians, performing good works to show our conversion. This is a fine thought at first glance, but shouldn't something happen to us before we start doing good works? When does faith enter the equation?

Here we begin to see the difference between faith and good works. Being "born anew" or "born from above" is not something we can do ourselves. It's a gift of the Holy Spirit, given through the miracle of Baptism and faith in Jesus Christ. Nicodemus is a pious man, and no doubt an expert in the law of God, but the law won't save him. Salvation comes from Christ alone, and this is the next thing that Jesus teaches Nicodemus. In a rather lengthy explanation, Jesus gives Nicodemus the basics of eternal life. To paraphrase, Jesus' message is this: *No one can go to heaven except through Me [Jesus Christ]. I'm giving up My life for the sins of the entire world. God the Father will sacrifice Me, His only Son, so that you won't have to pay for your own sins, a task which you could never accomplish. I'm giving you the faith, the salvation, and all of the gifts necessary to live eternally in heaven with Me. Many who hear this message will not take what is freely offered, but you must only receive this gift, and it will be yours*. This is one of the greatest passages in the entire Bible, and it includes a summary of the New Testament in one powerful verse. **"For God so loved the world that he gave his one and only Son, that whoever believes in him shall not perish but have eternal life"** (John 3:16). Remember this truth, believe in it, and you will be saved!

There it is. Nicodemus has now heard all that he needs to know. What will he do with this knowledge? What do *we* do, once we have heard the message of Jesus Christ? Should we be ashamed to spread this message? No! Note these words of Christ which are recorded in the Gospels of Luke and Mark: **"If anyone is ashamed of me and my words, the Son of Man will be ashamed of him when he comes in His glory and in the glory of the Father and of the holy angels"** (Luke 9:26). This warning is for everyone. Even if you have the peace and assurance of your own salvation, what about your neighbor? Don't you care about the condition of your neighbor's soul as well? We don't want to see anyone in danger of going to hell, but that's exactly what the future holds for those who reject and jeer at the saving Gospel message of Jesus Christ. Share the message, and don't be discouraged about how it's received. The Holy Spirit knows who will and who won't reject this message, and He always accomplishes His will.

This encounter between Nicodemus and Christ in the darkness is the most we see of Nicodemus in the entire Bible, although he does appear again briefly two more times. This story of one minor Pharisee is one of the most telling and clear arguments for baptism and belief in Christ throughout the Bible. When we leave Nicodemus here, however, he doesn't appear to be any different. So what happens to this curious man?

Four chapters later, we see that the Pharisees have grown tired of Jesus and His ministry. He's destroying their reputations as law-abiding and holy men, and telling the people that He's God! Just when they're about to sentence Jesus to death without trial, Nicodemus (yes, the same Nicodemus!) steps in and argues from their point of view (after all, he is himself a Pharisee). **"Nicodemus, who had gone to Jesus earlier and who was one of their own number, asked, 'Does our law condemn anyone without first hearing him to find out what he is doing?'"** (John 7:50-51). Now he hits them where it hurts, right in the law book. The Pharisees are left with only two options: give Christ a fair chance to speak His part, or break one of the laws that form the very foundation of their entire existence as men of the law. If Nicodemus had simply stepped in and said "I love Christ – He's my Savior! Don't speak in such a way about Him!" he would've been laughed out of the meeting and defrocked. But Nicodemus, under the auspicious eye of the law, sets up a legal barrier between Jesus and certain harm.

This is a great lesson in how we can use our own particular talents to make a case for Christ as well. I knew men at the seminary who had formerly been employed as engineers, teachers, lawyers, and factory workers. Each carried with him unique talents which could be used to further the cause of Christ. Many of them also had families full of individuals with their own talents and abilities. How about you? Maybe you're an office worker with great organizational skills, or perhaps an artist with incredible creativity. No matter what talents and gifts you have been endowed with, these can be used in your own witness and service as baptized Christians.

So is this the last time we hear of Nicodemus, or will we see him again? Has he truly changed, or is he just being fair to a Man who treated him with respect and kindness? To find out, we must go all the way to the end of Christ's ministry – after He has just been crucified. Joseph of Arimathea has asked for the body of Christ so that he may properly bury it. **"He was accompanied by Nicodemus, the man who earlier had visited Jesus at night. Nicodemus brought a mixture of myrrh and aloes, about seventy-five pounds"** (John 19:39). Why did Nicodemus bring such a great amount of myrrh and aloes? The New American Commentary sheds some light on the historical significance of this. *"It was truly an immense amount of spice. Indeed, it was enough spice to bury a king royally."*[3] Nicodemus has finally come to see Christ as the true King – a king whose kingdom isn't of this world, but of the heavens. Nicodemus desires to be one of those who can faithfully serve under Christ for all eternity, and although he and Joseph are still serving Christ in secret, they're doing a great deed for the kingdom of God.

As Christians, our service to the Lord manifests itself in many forms. Some are pastors, whose entire life is dedicated to maintaining a faithful calling to preach the Word and administer the Sacraments (Baptism, Communion, and Absolution).[4] Others serve Christ by sharing His message of salvation with co-workers, family members, and friends. There's no minimum or maximum amount of effort when it comes to faithfully serving Jesus. It is, however, the Holy Spirit working through the efforts of all of the "ordinary" people that makes the difference. We must never think that we can't make an impact on the kingdom of God, for this is entirely up to the Holy Spirit. If only the most devout and truly dedicated among us were worthy of the kingdom of

---

[3] Borchert, Gerald L. Vol. 25B, *John 12-21*. electronic ed. Logos Library System; The New American Commentary (p. 281). Nashville: Broadman & Holman, 2002.

[4] *The Book of Concord: The Confessions of the Evangelical Lutheran Church*, R. Kolb & T.J. Wengert, Eds. (p. 219). Minneapolis: Fortress, 2000.

God, we wouldn't know the story of Nicodemus at all, and my book would never have been written. Our lives are a testament to God's extraordinary grace!

Study Questions

Q1. Nicodemus has a chance to meet with Jesus Christ privately, face to face (**John 3:1-2**). What would you do or say if you had the chance to meet and speak with Jesus today?

Q2. What is Nicodemus's occupation (**3:1**)? What is the significance of his occupation to this narrative?

Q3. Read **John 3:3-8**. What does this conversation between Jesus and Nicodemus teach us about Baptism? What does this mean on page 75: "we actually die with Christ in our baptism and are raised to new life through the water and Word"? See also **Romans 6:3-4** and **Titus 3:4-7**.

Q4. On pages 75-76, I speak of the Holy Spirit's work in the conversion of sinners. What exactly is the work of the Holy Spirit? What is our role in the conversion of sinners and the spreading of God's Word? Read **1 Peter 3:15**.

Q5. Why is **John 3:16** often called the "Gospel in a nutshell"?

Solomon

37 "As the LORD was with my lord the king, so may he be with Solomon to make his throne even greater than the throne of my lord King David!" (1 Kings 1:37)

Anyone who's had some familiarity with Solomon or has studied him at all knows that Solomon doesn't seem like your ordinary guy. His father is none other than King David, the greatest king that Israel has ever known. This gives Solomon some rather large shoes to fill. Solomon's birth comes at a turbulent and dangerous time. David has sinned in the eyes of the Lord with Bathsheba, who was once the wife of Uriah. Although David's is a story for another time, this much is important to know: the Lord took David's firstborn from him. David has also seen his sin through the eyes of the prophet Nathan and knows that he deserves death. Because he repented and grieved over his sin, however, the Lord blessed him with a son who promises to be great. His name is Solomon.

What makes Solomon special? First of all, he is born with the Lord's blessing. **"Then David comforted his wife Bathsheba, and he went to her and lay with her. She gave birth to a son, and they named him Solomon. The LORD loved him"** (2 Samuel 12:24). Surely the Lord loves us all, but David's descendents have a special honor. One of them is to be the Messiah who will save all people from their sin. All signs at the time indicated that Solomon could and would be this Messiah.

Can you picture Solomon's upbringing? It would be difficult enough simply to be the king's son, but Solomon had the added pressure of being the supposed Messiah. I think Solomon's situation might be similar to that of a teenage film or pop star. They have so much pressure placed upon them to be perfect all of the time, and they often crack under that pressure. A similar example can be seen with children who have been very promising athletes from a young age. Some of these prodigies had parents who would squeeze every last bit of potential out of them before the kids eventually gave up on athletics altogether. They quit because they came to see it as a constant competition instead of a healthy lifestyle; and none of us can win all of the time. So what about Solomon? Did he crack under the immense pressure? Surprisingly, he did quite well – at least in the beginning.

How did Solomon end up as king if he wasn't the eldest brother? His older brother Adonijah (who was the son of Haggith and David, and perhaps David's oldest living son at this time), assumed that the throne was his for the taking, nearly putting an end to Solomon's bid before it began. Adonijah went so far as to make the sacrifices, hold the banquets, and even began to develop the following of a king of Israel. It appeared that Solomon, born of Bathsheba, would be treated as a second class citizen in his own household instead of assuming the throne. Fortunately, the influential men surrounding the great king David during his reign, not to mention Bathsheba (as we learned before with Esther, the wife of the king has incredible influence when she uses it!) had no intention of going against the Lord's will for His kingdom. In an amazing turn of events, recorded in 1 Kings 1:38-52, Solomon is immediately transformed from outcast son to mighty king of Israel. So great was the influence of these men, not to mention the pleasure of the crowds, that even David was forced to declare his allegiance to the new king. **"The king [David] bowed in worship on his bed and said, 'Praise be to the LORD, the God of Israel, who has allowed my eyes to see a successor on my throne today'"** (1 Kings 1:47-48). David, a king favored by the Lord, saw this as God's will and respectfully stepped aside for his young son, whom he hoped would one day become the Savior of Israel.

So what became of Adonijah? Did he intend to dispute Solomon's claims that he was the new king? **"Then Solomon was told, 'Adonijah is afraid of King Solomon and is clinging to the horns of the altar. He says, 'Let King Solomon swear to me today that he will not put his servant to death with the sword''"** (1 Kings 1:51). Adonijah, a powerful man by his own right, fully realized that he couldn't fight God's will for Israel. At this point, he was more concerned for his life, knowing that he was an imposter and that such treachery deserved death. Solomon, proving to be a fair and godly king, spared his brother's life and began his reign as king of Israel.

Solomon appears very much in control of his life at this point. Newly crowned, just as was foretold, he was about to receive a divine assignment from God. This would be like when Moses led Israel out of Egypt or when Noah built the Ark. As I mentioned before, David had done wrong in the eyes of the Lord with Bathsheba, who wasn't his wife at that time, and the Lord punished him for this. David was no longer worthy to build the temple of God. This temple, God's home on earth, would be built by the hands of Solomon, who had remained upright in the eyes of the Lord.

Imagine that Solomon's journey is similar to that of a child prodigy who goes on to earn great success in the world of sports. Perhaps a great high school basketball player is drafted right away to the NBA. Now he's king of his sport, at the very top. He continues to work hard and play well only to be rewarded with league MVP, making him the critic's choice for best player in the entire professional world of basketball. This kid may be only 20 years old, but he's considered the best of the best. What tremendous pressure that must be, with nowhere to go but down!

Now step outside that analogy again. A youth has just been promoted to king, which is magnificent in its own right, but now he is to be honored above any other man in the entire world by building the Lord's house on earth. Solomon, for the time being, is the most important man on earth. Now, that's pressure! In matters concerning the Lord, however, we know that men never actually accomplish what they are credited for; they simply let the Lord do His work. This is how the building of the temple would occur as well. **"Do not be afraid or discouraged, for the LORD God, my God, is with you. He will not fail you or forsake you until all the work for the service of the temple of the LORD is finished"** (1 Chronicles 28:20). David, a great hero of faith, encouraged his son to complete the task set before him, knowing that he would have all the help he needed. The Lord would be guiding him every step of the way. Along with his advice, David presented him with something slightly more specific. **"He [David] gave him [Solomon] the plans of all that the Spirit had put in his mind for the courts of the temple of the LORD and all the surrounding rooms, for the treasuries of the temple of God and for the treasuries for the dedicated things"** (1 Chronicles 28:12). The list doesn't stop there. The plans cover every single detail, down to the weight and amount of precious metals that would go into each facet of the temple. What is the most important thing for us to note about these plans? They're given directly by the Holy Spirit, who works in the hearts and minds of men to help them accomplish the Lord's will. Apart from the Spirit, Solomon could do nothing. However, with the Spirit's guidance, he couldn't fail. Or could he?

At first Solomon appeared to be taking this daunting task in stride; he carried out the Lord's (and his father's) wishes to the letter (**2 Chronicles 2:1; 3:1**) and he even managed to give credit where credit was due (**2 Chronicles 6:12-15**). Solomon pleased the Lord so greatly that He bestowed upon him yet another divine gift – He promised to give Solomon anything his heart desired. Solomon, with the opportunity to gain all the wealth and riches of the world, asked instead for wisdom. **"Give me wisdom and knowledge, that I may lead this people, for who is able to govern this great people of yours?"** (2 Chronicles 1:10). Because his request was so selfless, God granted him wealth and power along with unmatched wisdom. If you've ever heard of Solomon, you've certainly heard of his wisdom. At one point in my life, I knew nothing of Solomon other than the great wisdom that he possessed. Like Jonah with the great fish, this is one of those stories in Biblical history that sticks in our heads because of its extraordinary elements. No man possessed a wisdom like Solomon's. This great and mighty king would go on to solve many disputes and serve as a fair and honorable judge to his people. He even wrote several books of the Bible – Song of Solomon, Ecclesiastes, and Proverbs – as well as a few of the Psalms. The most intelligent scholars today still find it a challenge to fully understand this inspired and timeless knowledge. All of this magnificent wisdom was provided by the Lord, and this gift is just one more reason why Solomon should have been upright in every way. But he wasn't.

A proper study of Solomon should certainly include the temple which he built, along with his immense wealth and wisdom. However, to give a balanced and accurate assessment of this great man, we also need to mention Solomon's numerous sins and vices as he sat upon the throne of Israel. It's been said that "absolute power corrupts absolutely," and we see evidence of this all the time. From sexual affairs to the embezzlement of money, many politicians and other leaders create a scandalous mess, with little regard for others. For some people, the more power and responsibility you give them, the less they are capable of handling the pressure that accompanies it. This is true even when the Lord has promised to guide and help them along the way. **"God is faithful; he will not let you be tempted beyond what you can bear. But when you are tempted, he will also provide a way out so that you can stand up under it"** (1 Corinthians 10:13). We often ignore these words, trying to take matters into our own hands. This is why Christians fall under the pressures of the devil and the world as well. God constantly works with us, and we receive His mighty benefits and gifts, but we fall short. Solomon definitely fell short as well.

Solomon appeared to have everything that a man could ever want: power, riches, wisdom, faith – but this wasn't enough for him. Solomon sought to satisfy his appetite for pleasure in other ways as well. One of these pleasures was women. If you're like me, you find it a little disturbing when someone (usually a Mormon or Muslim) claims that they can have two wives. Biblical examples have shown us that when men – Abraham, Jacob, and David come to mind – have more than one wife, it can lead to despair and loads of trouble. But Solomon didn't simply take two wives, did he? **"Solomon held fast to them [his lovers] in love. He had seven hundred wives of royal birth and three hundred concubines"** (1 Kings 11: 2b-3a).   The situation that Solomon made for himself was literally a thousand women for one man. If he was to devote a day to each of them in succession, it would take nearly three years to see all of them! You may think you now understand why Solomon fell in the Lord's eyes, but it wasn't the wives.

The wives contributed to the real problem, but they weren't the problem themselves. If we read a bit further in this passage we can, however, locate the real source of the problem. **"He had seven hundred wives of royal birth and three hundred concubines, and his wives led him astray. As Solomon grew old, his wives turned his heart after other gods, and his heart was not fully devoted to the LORD his God, as the heart of David his father had been"**

(1 Kings 11:3-4). Herein lies the problem, and the most critical error that any Christian can make. Solomon began to worship the false gods of his wives instead of devoting himself fully to the Lord, who had given him everything in the first place. Which commandment did he break? He broke the most important of all the commandments – the first. **"I am the LORD your God, who brought you out of Egypt, out of the land of slavery. "You shall have no other gods before Me"** (Exodus 20:2-3).

Why is this commandment considered the most important one of all? Failing to fear, love, and trust in God above all things is the foothold to breaking all of the other commandments. Jesus also stresses the importance of the first commandment when He addresses the Pharisees on a question concerning the law: **"'Love the Lord your God with all your heart and with all your soul and with all your mind.' This is the first and greatest commandment"** (Matthew 22:37-38). Okay, so Solomon broke the commandment. He's still the richest, wisest man in the world, *and* king of Israel. What could possibly happen to him?

"So the LORD said to Solomon, 'Since this is your attitude and you have not kept my covenant and my decrees, which I commanded you, I will most certainly tear the kingdom away from you and give it to one of your subordinates. Nevertheless, for the sake of David your father, I will not do it during your lifetime. I will tear it out of the hand of your son. Yet I will not tear the whole kingdom from him, but will give him one tribe for the sake of David my servant and for the sake of Jerusalem, which I have chosen" (1 Kings 11:11-13). Solomon blew it, and he'll have to give up everything for his mistakes. However, because David was so pleasing in the eyes of the Lord, and because David never strayed from the eyes of the Lord (even in his sin), God lessens the severity of the punishment. David certainly was a sinner as well, but his repentance and dependence on the Lord was pleasing to God. Therefore, He allowed the kingdom to remain. Despite this, however, the remnant of the kingdom would undergo great pains in the process.

It's often painful when someone else pays for *our* mistakes; our fear mixes with shame as we see our rightful punishment falling upon them. Solomon wouldn't lose all of his riches and power, but neither would he be able to pass them on to his children. Israel would now be a land divided, and it would see much war and famine, even to the present day. But we should focus on the positive results of this action. God has kept one tribe under the house of Solomon. From this tribe would come many men and women of faith – men and women who would eventually lead to the promised Messiah. This Messiah is Jesus Christ, our Lord and Savior. This Messiah was born in a humble manger and lived His life in humility and suffering. This Messiah took upon Himself the sins of the entire world with His death and resurrection. Even though Solomon once ruined everything, Christ made it whole again – even better than before. Just as Solomon's children would pay for his sins, Christ paid the price for our sins as well.

I can think of no better way to close this chapter and remind you of Christ's provision for us than to share these comforting words from the mouth of our Savior. Here Jesus passionately tells God's children that even the most ordinary flowers are given as much attention and care as the greatest kings in their decadent splendor. We truly are equally loved in God's sight! **"See how the lilies of the field grow. They do not labor or spin. Yet I tell you that not even Solomon in all his splendor was dressed like one of these. If that is how God clothes the grass of the field, which is here today and tomorrow is thrown into the fire, will he not much more clothe you, O you of little faith? So do not worry, saying, 'What shall we eat?' or 'What shall we drink?' or**

'What shall we wear?' For the pagans run after all these things, and your heavenly Father knows that you need them. But seek first his kingdom and his righteousness, and all these things will be given to you as well. Therefore do not worry about tomorrow, for tomorrow will worry about itself. Each day has enough trouble of its own" (Matthew 6:28-34).

Study Questions

Q1. Read **2 Samuel 12:13-25**. Why was Solomon's birth such a blessed event? Also see page 83.

Q2. David's throne wasn't simply handed over to Solomon (see page 84). Who or what might have prevented Solomon from taking the throne of Israel (**1 Kings 1:5**)? Read **1 Kings 1:38-53**. How did Solomon overcome obstacles to his becoming king? Did Solomon's first act as king prove or disprove his worthiness for the crown?

Q3. God offers Solomon anything that his heart desires. Read **2 Chronicles 1:7-12**. What would you ask for? What does Solomon ask for? How does his request present a great model for our own prayers? See also **Matthew 21:22**.

Q4. Solomon appears to have everything going for him (**1 Chronicles 28:5-7**), until he falls. Read **1 Kings 11:1-13**. What is his greatest sin (see pages 88-89)? What commandments have been broken here? Do we fall victim to the same sins as Solomon? Why?

Q5. Sin has a price (**Romans 6:23**). Read **1 Kings 11:9-13**. Did Solomon have to pay the price for his own sins? Who *will* see the consequences of Solomon's shortcomings? Has anyone ever been punished for something that you did wrong?

Q6. See page 90. What, besides the temple, was Solomon's greatest legacy?

Q7. Read **Matthew 6:28-34**. Of what can we be certain in this life?

Zacchaeus

²A man was there by the name of Zacchaeus; he was a chief tax collector and was wealthy. ³He wanted to see who Jesus was, but being a short man he could not, because of the crowd. ⁴So he ran ahead and climbed a sycamore-fig tree to see him, since Jesus was coming that way. (Luke 19:2-4)

What makes a hero? The answer will depend on whom you ask. Some might say that police officers, fire fighters, and soldiers are heroes, because they put their lives on the line every day and fight for our freedom. Others might say that world class athletes are heroes because of their physical superiority and ability to inspire. Still others would give this title to those who faithfully serve us each day, such as our dedicated parents and teachers. If you're part of a church, you may see your pastor or other church workers as heroes. So what's our criterion for being a true hero? Where does Zacchaeus, the chief tax collector, fit in? If you've noticed any kind of common thread weaving itself through the characters of this book, it is a reliance upon God, and a trust that He will work in their lives. These ordinary people don't live perfect lives – they often fall and stumble along the way – but they are still heroes for trusting God. We also make mistakes in our walk with God, but this doesn't make us any less Christian. It certainly doesn't mean that we're not equally loved by Him. Zacchaeus learns this lesson while climbing trees.

Those of us who attended Sunday School when we were younger may remember a song that goes like this: *"Zacchaeus was a wee little man, a wee little man was he. He climbed up in a sycamore tree, for the Lord he wanted to see..."* The song is very simple, but it covers most of what

Zacchaeus is attributed with in the Bible. Let's not romanticize his role in the Scriptures; he's not in the same realm as a King David or a Moses, and yet God worked in Zacchaeus just as powerfully, and the deeds of Zacchaeus were every bit as pleasing to our Lord. So what did Zacchaeus do? Who is this guy?

I mentioned before that if the Gospel writers really wanted something to be remembered, it usually appears more than once between the four books – Matthew, Mark, Luke and John. Take, for instance, the feeding of the 5000 by Jesus. This occurs in each of the Gospels and is a crucial event in His ministry. Zacchaeus, on the other hand, is recorded only in the Gospel of Luke. His story is contained within ten verses, most of which are filled with the words of Christ. On the surface, it doesn't appear that Zacchaeus did anything noteworthy, but his story is indeed important. Zacchaeus was a tax collector by profession, one of the most despised of all occupations. His job, essentially, was to make sure that people were paying their tributes to King Herod. He was almost a reverse Robin Hood, taking from the poor and giving to the rich. While doing this, he also became quite wealthy.

Zacchaeus wasn't just any tax collector; he served as the chief tax collector in the city of Jericho, which was a well-known toll place in the area of Palestine. Zacchaeus is also the only person in the entire Bible who's identified as a chief tax collector, so we can assume he was quite wealthy and prominent in the community. As the chief tax collector, Zacchaeus would have been looked down upon by faithful Jews as a terrible sinner and a thief. We should look upon his role as a representation of all ordinary sinners responding to Jesus.

"He wanted to see who Jesus was, but being a short man he could not, because of the crowd. So he ran ahead and climbed a sycamore-fig tree to see him, since Jesus

was coming that way" (Luke 19:3-4). Zacchaeus is short, and while this has little impact on his character, it does give credibility to the fact that he had to climb a tree to see Jesus. Doesn't it seem strange that a man of status would climb a tree? Shouldn't he be able to simply elbow his way through the crowd by the authority of his position alone? Whether or not he could have used his position to get to the front of the line, he doesn't. His urgency to catch a glimpse of the Lord was so great that he resorted to climbing up a tree just to get a look at Him. Do we ever feel this urgency in our lives? We frequently do things that we're not proud of, and sometimes we do them as part of our profession. This day-to-day struggle within ourselves can push us right into the arms of our Savior (by the grace of the Holy Spirit), but it often pulls us in the other direction.

I used to work at a high-end clothing store. Our duty as sales representatives was to trick, scheme, flatter, and lie so that people would buy things that they didn't need. For instance, all of the mannequins in the store had to be "layered" so that several shirts and accessories were clearly visible. The underlying marketing procedure was to give the appearance that one shirt or bracelet couldn't be worn without the other items. Although a very simple concept, this method proved extremely successful in boosting commissions. Such tactics are not exclusive to the fashion industry, however, and most sales positions operate on the same idea. It was literally my job to get people to spend more money than they originally intended, or than they even had. Now imagine if your job was to take people's money for some grand building fund or simply the king's wishes, and they received nothing in return. At least those whom I sold clothing to were able to wear nice outfits afterwards. When Zacchaeus was done with someone, they could only look on as the rich got richer, and – well, you know the rest. He must have felt pangs of remorse for this way of life, and wanted to see the One who could

cleanse any leper and heal any disease, even death. Surely
this Jesus could help him as well!

**"When Jesus reached the spot, he looked up and
said to him, 'Zacchaeus, come down immediately. I must
stay at your house today.' So he came down at once and
welcomed him gladly. All the people saw this and began
to mutter, 'He has gone to be the guest of a 'sinner''"**
(Luke 19:5-7). Jesus was famous for associating with those
whom society rejected. In doing so, He became another
"rejected" member of society Himself. No self-respecting
Jew would stay with a hated crook and swindler like
Zacchaeus, and yet Jesus does. Christ explains these actions
in the fifth chapter of Luke when He is again dining with tax
collectors and other sinners. **"It is not the healthy who need
a doctor, but the sick. I have not come to call the righteous, but sinners to repentance"** (Luke 5:31-32). Christ is
on earth to minister to the sick and sinful – Zacchaeus
included.

Note what Zacchaeus does in response. He's overwhelmed and overjoyed that Jesus wants to stay with him.
He doesn't drag his feet or feel the need to explain to Jesus
what kind of scoundrel he's been. Ecstatic in Christ's presence, he is content to simply provide Him lodging and
fellowship. Zacchaeus provides a wonderful example for us
here. So many hesitate coming to Christ because they think
He won't want them; they are ashamed of all the things that
they've done in their past. But Christ is ready and willing to
accept them and us with open arms. When I decided to
become a pastor, I figured that I'd meet quite a bit of
resistance. After all, I didn't seem to fit the "profile" of a
holy man of God. This was the beginning, however, of my
understanding of God's desires for His servants. He calls
ordinary sinners, of whom I am one, to help with His work.
He uses us for His divine purposes, and much greatness can

come out of our less-than-perfect efforts. What God works through Zacchaeus next is nothing short of a miracle.

Tax collectors fulfilled their duty out of greed and love of state. They didn't think about others in the process. It's one of those jobs where if you stop to think about it, you're likely to feel the pangs of guilt. One can rationalize that it's better to take the money and move on. Zacchaeus has experienced a change within himself, however, and this becomes quite apparent through his next statement. **"Zacchaeus stood up and said to the Lord, 'Look, Lord! Here and now I give half of my possessions to the poor, and if I have cheated anybody out of anything, I will pay back four times the amount'"** (Luke 19:8). Just this short amount of time with Jesus has helped Zacchaeus to see that his lifestyle is contrary to Jesus' preaching and teaching. He is ready to live his life for Christ and his neighbor. He'll certainly stumble along the way, but he's off to a good start. He's promised to give his excess money to those who can use it, and he's going to make reparations to those whom he's swindled. This is the beginning of a new life for Zacchaeus. His life will now be lived for others, centered on Christ and His teachings.

Zacchaeus' amazing transformation serves as a terrific model in our own Christian walk. Most of us have done things in the past of which we are not proud. In my own past, there was a time when I had fallen into a self-created pit of loneliness and deception. However, after Christ plucked me out from the abyss of despair, I felt renewed and motivated to make changes in my life. Certainly, God is pleased with faithful belief and humble lives given to Him in service. However, going the extra mile to repair past mistakes – such as Zacchaeus promises to Christ – is a terrific Christian witness to others.

In my own reparations, I didn't give a fortune away to others, but I did apologize for any hurt I might have caused them. Since I was willing to do this, God blessed me many times over, working in the hearts of past friends and acquaintances to quickly forgive me and allow me back into their lives. They noticed the change that God worked in me, and I have been overwhelmed by the amount of respect and kindness that characterizes our patched relationships. It's not always this easy, and God certainly doesn't expect us to give everything away. However, this sacrificial love provides the most natural witness that any of us can achieve. Zacchaeus realized this as well, and the fortune that he subsequently gave away must have proved a powerful example of the changing power of Christ's love. Grace *is* amazing, and as Christians, our love speaks volumes more about our relationship with God than any amount of strict obedience could ever hope to accomplish.

Christ closes this section of the Bible by stating His purpose for Zacchaeus. **"Today salvation has come to this house, because this man, too, is a son of Abraham. For the Son of Man came to seek and to save what was lost"** (Luke 19:9-10). Even Zacchaeus – just like each of us wretched sinners – is a sheep in Christ's fold. As our Faithful Shepherd, Christ will neither leave nor forsake us. Zacchaeus is a true "son of Abraham," because He realizes who Abraham's Father is – none other than Jesus Christ.

So what's our definition of a hero? Certainly we can see firefighters, police officers, pastors, teachers, soldiers, and parents as heroes, but the real hero is the one who believes in Christ's extraordinary message and lives his or her life for Him. We are part of the redeemed, and as such we're blessed to live our lives in service to Christ. He has paid the price of our sins in full, and we're the benefactors. Zacchaeus, despite his past, knew this and clung to it. He's a true hero of the faith.

Study Questions

Q1. On page 95, we read that it takes more than an occupation to make someone a "hero." Who are your heroes? What makes a real hero? Read **Philippians 4:13**.

Q2. Zacchaeus has a very special occupation (**Luke 19:2**). What does he do for a living?

Q3. What does the tree climbing incident teach us about Zacchaeus (**Luke 19:3-4**)? Read **Luke 5:31-32**. How do our shortcomings and mistakes show us a need for a Savior? Paul offers us insight in **2 Corinthians 12:9-10**.

Q4. See page 99. What do Zacchaeus' actions teach us about the nature of true repentance (**Luke 19:8**)?

Q5. What does Christ mean by calling Zacchaeus a "son of Abraham" (**Luke 19:9-10**)? Are we also sons of Abraham?

Rahab

¹⁷ The city and all that is in it are to be devoted to the LORD. Only Rahab the prostitute and all who are with her in her house shall be spared, because she hid the spies we sent. (Joshua 6:17)

What motivates us to come to God? While we'd love to think that some great inner desire to serve the Lord will come upon us one day, another likely reason that you came to God (or will in the future) is that you were afraid. When was it that you finally believed in hell? What was once a distant and figurative punishment in our minds now becomes a very real consequence of disobedience, and we're terrified. Some don't realize their fear of hell and eternal punishment until their deathbeds. We can thank all of the wonders of modern science for such a literal view of life – one lacking in spirituality and faith.

In today's society, it's becoming increasingly difficult to believe in things that we cannot touch, taste, and smell. We fool around and seek empty pleasures our entire lives, never worrying about the ramifications – that is, until something tragic happens, and the safe existence that we imagined for ourselves is snatched away. Perhaps you have experienced an untimely death in your family or maybe even a murder. The frailty of human life becomes all too real when we are presented with the reality of death. Anyone who has witnessed a car accident or a near drowning knows that life can be snuffed out in the blink of an eye. What awaits us after death? Once we start pondering this question in earnest, we're thrust into the reality of the Bible and its promises. We read that we *will* go to hell if we don't believe in Jesus Christ as our Savior. When this becomes true to us through our exposure to God's Word, we each are faced with this incredible reality: believe in Jesus Christ for the salvation of our soul or go to hell. There is no gray area, and the consequences are eternal.

The good news is that once the fear of hell has crept into our minds, we want to find out more about this Jesus Christ who is constantly seeking us to save our lives for eternity. How can He do this? How is it possible? This is the beginning of faith, and believe it or not, Christ brings this faith to you, not the other way around. I mentioned earlier that I wasn't seeking Christ when He found me. I wouldn't have come to Him on my own – period.

One of Jesus' ancestors, who is credited throughout the Bible for her faith, came to believe in God through fear. After coming to an understanding of the grace that was hers through the One True God, she finally came to fear the God of the Jews as a child fears a parent. Rahab, the celebrated ally of God in the Old Testament, started out pretty ordinary. Calling any prostitute "ordinary" is a stretch, but she was indeed just a common person – a sinner among many in the city of Jericho.

Rahab was fortunate to receive faith when she did, for many reasons. God placed certain events in her life to bring her to this reality, but what if she had continued to reject Him? She'd be one among many who faced the fires of eternal punishment. But her story didn't take such a downward turn. On the contrary, Rahab responded to her call to faith in the best possible way. As previously mentioned, Rahab was a prostitute. Perhaps she is more accurately portrayed as an innkeeper, but we won't attempt to glamorize her profession. She may have owned a business on the side, but she was definitely a prostitute by today's standards. We're not given enough information to know for sure, but the wording used causes us to believe that she led a very undesirable and isolated existence. She sounds like a perfect candidate for God's extraordinary grace, doesn't she?

Rahab's story begins with Joshua, the great warrior and successor of Moses, as he is dispatched to Jericho. Soon the Lord will allow the tremendous and formidable walls of Jericho to shatter at no more than the blast of trumpets. Joshua sent two spies into town, where they decided to stay with Rahab. We can assume that these holy warriors wouldn't seek out a prostitute's comfort; it is more likely that Rahab had some kind of accommodations for travelers. Thus she took them in and cared for them. Whether by some mistake on their part or by simple treachery, Joshua's spies were discovered and the king of Jericho (the enemy) was informed of their whereabouts. Immediately, Rahab was sought out for instruction by the king. Picture a simple innkeeper thrust into the center of an epic battle with both sides depending on her for military leverage. It sounds like a plot in a movie. She carries the fate of Joshua's spies in her ordinary hands, and now the king of her city is looking for a personal favor.

"So the king of Jericho sent this message to Rahab: 'Bring out the men who came to you and entered your house, because they have come to spy out the whole land.'" (Joshua 2:3). Here's a cliffhanger! Rahab now had to decide between love of country and loyalty to these strangers in her household. Not only were her business and lifestyle at the mercy of the city's king, but these spies would be no match for the city's guard. The easy solution would be to rat them out. **"But the woman [Rahab] had taken the two men and hidden them. She said, 'Yes, the men came to me, but I did not know where they had come from. At dusk, when it was time to close the city gate, the men left. I don't know which way they went. Go after them quickly. You may catch up with them.'"** (Joshua 2:4-5). The next verses after these reveal that she had taken immediate action to help the spies. Rahab has now aided and abetted two fugitives, and her life will be worthless in the city of Jericho when she's discovered. What could have motivated her to take such daring action?

Earlier we noted the motivation of fear and its effectiveness in bringing us to God. We have a tendency to think of this fear in human terms and trivialize the results, but God works in ways we cannot understand. He knows that even in fear, we are learning to trust and love. But how does Rahab justify her treason against Jericho? **"I know that the LORD has given this land to you and that a great fear of you has fallen on us, so that all who live in this country are melting in fear because of you"** (Joshua 2:9). Here we see her reasoning. She saw God's hand in these men and their work. She also saw her mighty city clenched in fear. They were terrified of what might befall them if they stood against those whom the Lord favors. She too had felt this great fear of opposing God and admitted to the spies that her land belongs to the God of Israel (and His people). Only a fool would stand against the God of Israel, and she was beginning to see the big picture.

We wouldn't necessarily think of prostitutes and harlots as an intelligent and learned group. As a society, we tend to think that anyone in such a profession must lack the skills and intellect to find a more traditional occupation. Rahab, however, displays genius and foresight in her next statement to the spies: **"Now then, please swear to me by the LORD that you will show kindness to my family, because I have shown kindness to you. Give me a sure sign that you will spare the lives of my father and mother, my brothers and sisters, and all who belong to them, and that you will save us from death"** (Joshua 2:12-13). Perhaps Rahab was familiar with the account of Sodom and Gomorrah, the evil cities that the Lord burned to the ground in the book of Genesis. The few in those cities who actually trusted in God were spared, and all saved were of the family of Lot, the nephew of Abraham the patriarch. Rahab was probably familiar with this legendary tale and hoped it could happen for her. She has already displayed a working knowledge of God and His ways in her speech to the spies. She was now hoping that a righteous God would spare those who trust in Him. Her instincts prove correct, and the spies willingly accept her offer. However, Rahab's role in this story isn't quite done.

The spies then informed her that if she should break her part of the deal, the agreement would be nullified. She would also have to gather her family together. **"If anyone goes outside your house into the street, his blood will be on his own head; we will not be responsible. As for anyone who is in the house with you, his blood will be on our head if a hand is laid on him"** (Joshua 2:19). Rahab now has to concentrate her efforts on bringing her family together. In doing so, she runs the risk of exposing her treasonous behavior and putting her entire family in mortal danger. However, if she proves brave and cunning enough to accomplish this feat, her family will be protected. The spies tell her that they will provide the protection, but Rahab trusts that the Lord Himself will provide all that she needs. Rahab is now demonstrating an increasingly active and mature faith. She has moved from fear into action, openly defying the pagan city of Jericho, her home until now. This was the point of no return.

The story of Rahab is just a small tale inside the greater narrative of Israel's capturing of Jericho. The Bible doesn't even mention Rahab or her family again for several chapters. During this lull, many great events come to pass that change the face of history and bring about the miraculous fall of the walls of Jericho, which just happened to be the strongest and thickest around. In the midst of the fighting and subsequent destruction of this great city, Joshua remembered his promise. **"Then they burned the whole city and everything in it…but Joshua spared Rahab the prostitute, with her family and all who belonged to her, because she hid the men Joshua had sent as spies to Jericho – and she lives among the Israelites to this day"** (Joshua 6:24-25). Rahab's faith was simple, like that of a child. She feared God's wrath and she was compelled by His love and mercy. God, in turn, not only remembered Rahab, but blessed her with one of the greatest honors in all of history – including her in the lineage of Christ. The phrase "happily ever after" never appears in the Bible, but Rahab gets close, and we can appreciate the positive tone that ends this narrative.

Not all who come to faith will encounter such a happy ending here on earth. In fact, history is full of martyrs who are slain in God's name because they were bold enough to profess their faith. They need not fear, however, because their reward is eternal, and far greater than any earthly treasure. Christ says: **"Do not store up for yourselves treasures on earth, where moth and rust destroy, and where thieves break in and steal. But store up for yourselves treasures in heaven, where moth and rust do not destroy, and where thieves do not break in and steal. For where your treasure is, there your heart will be also"** (Matthew 6:19-21).

It's important to remember that even if Rahab had died in the midst of Jericho's fall, she still would have inherited eternal life. We must not be afraid to do the right thing at all times, even when it means that we will face negative consequences – whether it be scorn, punishment, or even death. God desires unwavering obedience, even in the midst of overwhelming circumstances, when we are tempted to simply compromise our faith by downplaying, hiding, or even denying it. Instead, we must always stand firm, knowing that God takes the stand *for* us. A strong, abiding faith that God will sustain His children in the midst of every danger makes all of us ordinary people truly extraordinary. Rahab is mentioned again at the very beginning of the New Testament, in the genealogy of Jesus Christ. She is one of three women to be mentioned in the genealogy of our Savior, one of the highest honors in the entire Bible. Her faith is remembered in the book of Hebrews (**11:31**) and James (**2:25**) as well.

Rahab was certainly a bold advocate for the Lord. She learned that God's enemies perished and that His children were cared for. She decided that she'd rather stay alive on the side of power than perish on the side of destruction. Harboring the spies and making the deal were situations that the Lord presented to her in order to secure her safety. What was once fear is now active faith. God has allowed Rahab to become a central figure in the Bible because He wants us to understand how normal His children really are. Amazing things happen to ordinary people because the Lord wills it in their lives. No amount of positive thinking or self-help could have saved Rahab from certain death. Only a blind and trusting faith in the Lord saw her through, and she'll enjoy the benefits of this forever.

Study Questions

Q1. On pages 103-104, I allude to a fear of hell driving Rahab (and us) into the arms of our Savior. Read **Galatians 2:16** and **Hebrews 10:1-4**. Can the law of God (fear of punishment) truly bring us to faith? If not, what does bring us to faith?

Q2. See page 104. Here we read about Rahab and her fear of God. Is it bad to fear God? Read **Proverbs 9:10** and also **2 Corinthians 7:1**. If the fear of God is *not* inherently evil, then what is the proper way to fear Him? Read **Hebrews 12:4-11**.

Q3. See pages 105-106. When Rahab is questioned regarding housing Joshua's spies (who were the enemies of Jericho), she has a difficult decision to make (**Joshua 2:1-3**). Have you ever had to choose between doing what is easy and what is right? Read **Joshua 2:9-11**. Why does Rahab make her final decision to side with Joshua and his God?

Q4. On page 108, we read that Rahab had faith like a child, and that this faith saved her. Read **Matthew 18:1-6**. Surely children are blessed in God's sight. If this is true, then what does Paul mean in **1 Corinthians 13:11** when he tells us to put off our childish ways?

Q5. Rahab's story has a happy ending (**Joshua 6:25**). Do all believers live "happily ever after" in this life? Why or why not? Read **John 15:18-25** and also **John 16:20-22**.

Hannah

¹⁰ In bitterness of soul Hannah wept much and prayed to the LORD. ¹¹ And she made a vow, saying, "O LORD Almighty, if you will only look upon your servant's misery and remember me, and not forget your servant but give her a son, then I will give him to the LORD for all the days of his life, and no razor will ever be used on his head." (1 Samuel 1:10-11)

How do you know when you've hit rock bottom? Is it when you don't want to roll out of bed in the morning because there just isn't any reason to get up? What sparks such depression in our lives? Surely tragedies come in all shapes and sizes, but when these events include our families, they're often escalated to a level that few can understand unless they've experienced it themselves. Hannah knew this grief – the inescapable sorrow and depression that wash over a person like black waves of distress. Hannah was the wife of Elkanah, a man that you have probably never heard of. Thus, Hannah is a virtually unknown woman from an unknown family. Like other characters in this study, her name isn't on the tip of your tongue. It's difficult to place where you've heard of her. One of the scariest things in life is being completely unknown. We get the feeling that not only did Hannah realize this fear, but she agonized over it. She even began to think that God had forgotten about her as well.

Being a wife has its privileges, but less so if you're only one of two wives, as was common in Hannah's time. While Elkanah's other wife, Peninnah, bore him children, Hannah was barren. A wife's ability to bear many children was a great measure of status in ancient Biblical times, especially if those children were strong and healthy sons.

Elkanah should have been very grateful for the children Peninnah bore him, but he loved Hannah more. Despite her closed womb, Hannah appeared to be her husband's favorite. **"To Hannah he gave a double portion because he loved her, and the LORD had closed her womb"** (1 Samuel 1:5). Spousal favoritism in polygamous relationships – even toward the barren wife – is a common theme in the Old Testament. Beginning with Abraham and Sarah (who didn't bear Isaac until she was ninety), continuing with Jacob and Rachel (who died giving birth to her second child later in life), and continuing further with Hannah. A husband's love for his wife, no matter how strong, is no guarantee that she will bear him children. Only the Lord can provide such things. Sometimes, the things we desire the most are also the hardest to obtain. This is part of God's plan for our lives. Would we truly know how to trust and be grateful if we received everything we wanted? Obviously, we wouldn't, and so God refines us by making us work and wait for our precious treasures here on earth.

How did Hannah respond to her situation? Elkanah had shown her every kindness, but her fellow wife, Peninnah, treated her miserably: **"And because the LORD had closed her womb, her rival kept provoking her in order to irritate her. This went on year after year. Whenever Hannah went up to the house of the LORD, her rival provoked her till she wept and would not eat"** (1 Samuel 1:6-7). Here we see a very human and vulnerable side of Hannah, and quite a few of us can relate to her reaction. After all, it wasn't her fault that she was barren. Nowadays, as in Biblical times, there are many women who are unable to bear children, and it remains an unfortunate reality. However, society's opinion of large families appears to have changed, and infertility is viewed as less of a stigma. For instance, the ideal household unit in our society today seems to be a small family with one or two children, thriving economically and living the "perfect life." It was quite the opposite in Biblical times, and large families were a source of pride. Having children would have been ideal for Hannah, and yet there she was, barren and scorned by her competitor.

Picturing wives in constant competition for the affections of a single husband is a terrible thought indeed, but it was Hannah's reality. God did not intend for men to marry multiple partners, which is made clear in the very first book of the Bible with the very first couple, Adam and Eve. **"A man will leave his father and mother and be united to his wife, and they will become one flesh"** (Genesis 2:24). A wife afflicted with any biological problem rendering her childless presents a difficult situation, but what if there is another wife in the mix as well? A man's natural tendency, in most situations, will be to favor the wife without the problems. Hannah had her husband's attention, but she also received a great deal of attention from the other wife, who constantly made her miserable. Year after year she was treated in this manner. The greatest blessing the Lord could have provided Hannah would have been a child, and yet she remained without even a glimmer of hope.

In her grief, Hannah went off by herself to seek comfort in the Lord. **"In bitterness of soul Hannah wept much and prayed to the LORD. And she made a vow, saying, 'O LORD Almighty, if you will only look upon your servant's misery and remember me, and not forget your servant but give her a son, then I will give him to the LORD for all the days of his life'"** (1 Samuel 1:10-11). Hannah's demonstration of prayer should serve as an example in our own prayer life. The text tells us that she was bitter and weeping as she prayed. God knows our hearts and will give to us according to our sincerity and actual need, for He knows our needs far better than we ever could. Hannah addressed God by His formal name, expressed her humility, and committed herself to God's loving care. This pattern clearly shows her understanding of God's will for his children. Even in such a pious and holy state, Hannah suffered more ridicule and embarrassment. Eli, the priest, saw her praying but didn't recognize what she was doing. **"Eli observed her mouth. Hannah was praying in her heart, and her lips were moving but her voice was not heard. Eli thought she was drunk and said to her, 'How long will you keep on getting drunk? Get rid of your wine'"** (1 Samuel 1:12-14). While Hannah's bitter weeping was touching enough to play even the hardest heartstrings, now we can add to her hopelessness two more woes: public embarrassment and false accusations. This is rock bottom.

Honorably, Hannah took the accusation in stride. I think that is all she could have done at this point. When I found myself friendless and nearly alone in college, all I could do was look up from the pit of my despair and see any change as positive. I chose to be honest with those whom I cared about. Hannah did the same. God rewarded us both with exactly what we needed. How did she respond to this ignorant priest? **"I have not been drinking wine or beer; I was pouring out my soul to the LORD. Do not take your servant for a wicked woman; I have been praying here out of my great anguish and grief"** (1 Samuel 1:15-16). With humility, Hannah stated her case before Eli, who granted that her request would be fulfilled. How can he say this? As God's representative, he can certainly provide comfort and words of wisdom, but only God can open Hannah's womb.

The exact amount of time before Hannah had her first child, Samuel, is unknown. God remembers her petition the very next day, so it's possible that she conceived within 24 hours of her prayer. Here's the kicker – even though Hannah had now given birth to a child, she had to give him up according to her promise to the Lord (**1 Samuel 1:11**) or risk provoking the wrath and anger of God. Who does Hannah love more? Will it be the son she never had until now, or the

God who opened her womb in the first place? It seems like an easy answer, but could you give up your child? This is no accidental birth. Hannah had been dreaming of her son from the very beginning, and now he was with her. This son is a miraculous gift, but now she must give him up. **"When the man Elkanah went up with all his family to offer the annual sacrifice to the LORD and to fulfill his vow, Hannah did not go. She said to her husband, 'After the boy is weaned, I will take him and present him before the LORD, and he will live there always'"** (1 Samuel 1:21-22).

This is why I love these studies so much – some of the greatest acts of faith in the entire Bible occur in the lives of Biblical characters who we know the least about. Hannah's son, Samuel, will go on to be a great judge and major figure of the Old Testament. He'll be important enough to have two books of the Bible named after him, which makes him the only person in the entire Old Testament to have this distinction. Abraham the Patriarch will always be remembered for his willingness to sacrifice his son Isaac to the Lord, but here Hannah is displaying a radical faith as well. Her son, like Abraham's, is long-awaited. Abraham, however, knew that the Lord would provide him a son somehow if his bloodline was to multiply: **"Abraham reasoned that God could raise the dead, and figuratively speaking, he did receive Isaac back from death"** (Hebrews 11:19). Hannah knew no such thing. This might be her only child. She was willing to become little more than a friend or an acquaintance to her only son – her miracle child – by giving him up to the Lord. She did it nonetheless, and through such a selfless act, this ordinary woman proved herself one of the most faithful characters in the entire Bible.

Hannah then weaned her infant son, and immediately brought him to the temple. She didn't hesitate to give to the Lord what belonged to Him. From this point on, Samuel would live permanently in the temple, never again with his earthly parents. As a boy dedicated to the service of God Almighty, he would also be raised by the priest – in this case, Eli. After explaining to Eli once again who she was and why she was there, Hannah began to pray. This next section is one of the lengthiest monologues of any character in the Bible, and certainly the most significant by a minor Bible character such as Hannah. This is where we truly see Hannah break from her shell of distress and sorrow and burst forth with joy and passion through prayer. The first few words of this prayer can be paralleled with quotations from well-known Biblical personalities from elsewhere in the Bible. **"My heart rejoices in the LORD; in the LORD my horn is lifted high. My mouth boasts over my enemies, for I delight in your deliverance"** (1 Samuel 2:1). What beautiful and God-pleasing poetry! Hannah, showing no signs of sorrow, knew her blessings and was thankful for them. We see very similar confessions from King David after the defeat of the giants in **2 Samuel 22** and also in the words of the Virgin Mary at the beginning of the Gospel of Luke. In each of these instances, great joy is being proclaimed, but Hannah's situation is a little different. When David sang these lines (this is more than mere speaking, for such poetry could only be sung) he had just experienced a great victory in the Lord. When Mary sang them, she had just been told that she was to be the mother of her Savior Jesus Christ. God was literally going to be born from her womb! No greater honor has been bestowed upon a human being. But Hannah was about to lose her son – not to death, but to service. She wouldn't be able to enjoy his company on a regular basis. She would no longer be like a mother, but an aunt at best.

Could you give up your child? What if you had been barren for years, only to receive the miracle of parenthood? Most of us couldn't fathom the extreme sorrow that must have characterized Hannah from the time she weaned Samuel until she left him with Eli, the priest. She must have felt a great emptiness inside her, consoled only by her faith in the Lord and the love of her husband. Despite this, and perhaps because of it, Hannah sang out in beautiful prayer and praise to her God. She understood that Samuel was a gift from God, and that she had no right to keep him. She also knew that God's will for her and her son was of the highest priority. We can also praise God in the midst of our darkest hour, knowing that all good things come from Him alone. Faith will bind all wounds and sustain us throughout our journey through this valley of the shadow of death (**Psalm 23:4**).

The nature of Hannah's relationship with Samuel is difficult to ascertain from the Bible's testimony, but certain passages hint at their love. **"Each year his [Samuel's] mother made him a little robe and took it to him when she went up with her husband to offer the annual sacrifice"** (1 Samuel 2:19). Except for these annual visits, the text implies that she never saw or interacted with her son. Since there was no post office, e-mail, or telephone in those days, the best she could hope for was that he'd be glad to see her when she made her annual trip. Hannah is only mentioned once more in the Bible, and Samuel isn't part of that account. He would go on to accomplish many great and marvelous things for the Lord, but she would merely be an afterthought.

Hannah's great example of humility and thankfulness should inspire us to put the very best construction on problems or obstacles that occur in our lives. God is in charge of everything, and while He never intends to hurt us, sometimes these obstacles can make us miserable because of our sinful existence. Because sin is so prevalent in the world and in our own flesh, any oppression we experience often feels like more than we can bear. However, God will provide a way out, as Paul says in his first letter to the Corinthian church: **"No temptation has seized you except what is common to man. And God is faithful; he will not let you be tempted beyond what you can bear. But when you are**

tempted, he will also provide a way out so that you can stand up under it" (1 Corinthians 10:13). Hannah knew this, or at least she hoped she did, and the Lord provided for her, making her a great example for men and women alike.

So what ever happened to Hannah, the great poet and mother of the Old Testament? She never received mention in the New Testament for her faith, but God blessed her in another way. Remember the woman who couldn't bear a child? God decided to change all of that, blessing her with a wonderful and satisfying end. The very priest who accused Hannah of drunkenness at the beginning, Eli, would be the one to finally bless her through the Lord. **"Eli would bless Elkanah and his wife [each year], saying, 'May the LORD give you children by this woman to take the place of the one she prayed for and gave to the LORD'"** (1 Samuel 2:20). God never leaves us empty-handed, and Hannah would prove to be no different. **"The LORD was gracious to Hannah; she conceived and gave birth to three sons and two daughters"** (1 Samuel 2:21). The answer to years of prayer would finally come true in God's time. Hannah was now the mother of six, the loving wife of Elkanah her husband, and a dedicated servant of the Lord. Her life had gone from the very depths of despair to the pinnacle of paradise. Trust in the Lord and His promises, and you too can experience the guidance of our Guardian and Redeemer Jesus Christ, the only true joy. These miracles are not limited to people in the Bible. They occur everyday in our lives as well. The same God who provided for Hannah still provides for you and me, and He will never leave our side: **"Be strong and courageous. Do not be afraid or terrified...for the LORD your God goes with you; he will never leave you nor forsake you"** (Deuteronomy 31:6). Glory be to God!

Study Questions

Q1. See page 113. The first part of Hannah's life was very difficult (**1 Samuel 1:1-16**). There had to be times when she felt that everyone, even God, had forgotten her. Do you ever feel like God has forgotten about you? Read **Deuteronomy 31:8** and **Jeremiah 29:11**. Is it possible that God could ever forget us?

Q2. In the midst of her prayer and sorrow, Eli intercedes to make Hannah even more miserable. Although she had reached rock bottom, Hannah responds with respect and dignity to Eli's accusation of drunkenness (**1 Samuel 1:15-16**). How does Hannah's behavior mirror Christ's own behavior? Read **Isaiah 53:7**. What can we learn from this?

Q3. See page 117. Hannah's life was little more than a blip on the radar of Samuel's life. Do you ever feel like you're in the supporting cast for someone else's story? Read **Matthew 10:29-30**. Is this the reality?

Q4. Hannah can teach us quite a bit about prayer (pages 115, 116, and 118). God has provided us with such terrific examples to follow! Read **1 Samuel 1:10-11** and also **2:1-11**. What specific elements of prayer do you see in Hannah's own prayers? Read **Matthew 21:21-22**. What is the power of prayer?

Q5. See page 117. How is Hannah's sacrifice of Samuel similar to Abraham's willingness to sacrifice Isaac?

Q6. How did God reward Hannah for her obedience (see page 120)? Did she live the rest of her years without any children, barren and alone?

Q7. Is Hannah the only person throughout the Bible to be richly blessed after a period of trials and suffering? Read **Job 42:10-17**. Of what can we be certain?

The Widow of Zarephath

[25] There were many widows in Israel in Elijah's time, when the sky was shut for three and a half years and there was a severe famine throughout the land. [26] Yet Elijah was not sent to any of them, but to a widow in Zarephath in the region of Sidon. (Luke 4:25-26)

When was the last time you were at the end of your rope? What causes your nerves to completely frazzle, and brings you to your breaking point? Picture yourself on the interstate, driving alone at night, in the rain, when suddenly your tire goes flat. You realize that repairing it will take some effort; it's dark outside, raining miserably, and all you have is that cheap little jack that comes with the car. This isn't going to be a quick and easy fix, and you're going to get drenched and filthy in the process. I remember a difficult period in my life when I was completely stressed out from juggling several important events all at once. I was trying to coordinate my graduation day, figure out which seminary I was going to attend, study for my college finals, and train for the conference track championships – which, unfortunately, were scheduled for the same day as graduation. If anyone had asked me to add one more thing onto my overflowing schedule, I probably would have snapped. When you're under this much stress, you don't feel like you have anything left to give. But I've only spoken of car troubles and college finals, not life and death situations. What if, by granting one more favor, you knew that you would not only be burdened but perhaps even die? Now imagine that the person in need of such a favor was a complete stranger. What would you do?

The widow who lived in Zarephath will not be remembered for her wealth, intelligence, or talents. She will forever be remembered for the kindness she showed to a stranger when she was at the limits of her ability to give. This woman, who is little more than a side note in the account of the Old Testament prophet Elijah, showed a kindness worthy of mention, even in the Bible.

So where is Zarephath, and who *is* this widow? *"Zarephath is located in Phoenicia, the very heart of Baalism."*[5] Phoenicia, located just west of the Mediterranean Sea, near modern day Tel-Aviv, was a hotspot for Baal worshipers and would not have been very hospitable for Elijah (who was an Israelite). Baalism was the worship of any number of pagan deities who supposedly controlled one or more aspects of life, such as weather, fertility, or agriculture. So why would Elijah come here in the first place? Immediately preceding this narrative, we see that Elijah had been in hiding, due to the fact that he had so outraged the evil Queen Jezebel that she had put a price on his head (**1 Kings 19:2-3**). As the spokesman for Almighty God, Elijah was perceived as a threat and an enemy by this pagan ruler. Because he could no longer enter the towns openly, he was drinking from a brook and being fed miraculously by ravens (**1 Kings 17:4-6**). However, a severe drought had gripped the area, and so this brook eventually dried up, leaving Elijah without a water supply. The Lord, ever providing for his servant, sent him to a place where finding hospitality was unlikely. **"Go at once to Zarephath of Sidon and stay there. I have commanded a widow in that place to supply you with food"** (1 Kings 17:9). It

---

[5] House, Paul R. Vol. 8, *1, 2 Kings*. electronic ed. Logos Library System; The New American Commentary (p. 214). Nashville: Broadman & Holman, 2001, c1995.

should be noted that this widow of Zarephath wasn't a believer in the One True God. She was just another pagan, living in a pagan area. The chances of Elijah receiving any hospitality from her were slim to none. So why would the Lord send him there? **"So he [Elijah] went to Zarephath. When he came to the town gate, a widow was there gathering sticks. He called to her and asked, 'Would you bring me a little water in a jar so I may have a drink?' As she was going to get it, he called, 'And bring me, please, a piece of bread'"** (1 Kings 17:10-11). Note that the widow didn't hesitate to accommodate this stranger's request for water, even though there was a shortage due to the drought. But now this man of God was asking even more from a poor widow – food from her cupboard, which was no doubt barren as a result of her station in life and the drought. How did she respond to this request? **"'As surely as the LORD your God lives,' she replied, 'I don't have any bread – only a handful of flour in a jar and a little oil in a jug. I am gathering a few sticks to take home and make a meal for myself and my son, that we may eat it – and die'"** (1 Kings 17:12). Enough is enough, and when survival becomes a struggle, the requests of strangers cannot be accommodated. This wasn't a heroic struggle for life, either. It was a de-pressed recognition of inevitable starvation, which had come slowly and painfully due to the drought. *"The drought has reduced her resources to a bit of flour, a dab of oil, and a few sticks of wood. She expects to starve to death along with her son."*[6] This was a woman beaten down by life, and her god Baal hadn't been able to provide for her. The "piece of bread" that Elijah asked for wouldn't simply deplete a portion of what she had left. It would wipe out her food supply

---

[6] House, 215.

completely. She and her son would both die in service to this unknown man.

There are several items worthy of mention at this point. First, the widow is young. We can assume this because her son is later referred to as a boy (**1 Kings 17:21**). We're talking about a woman who is probably in her twenties or thirties. We also notice that her son isn't helping her gather sticks, even though she is about to die from the effort. Since no honorable son would allow his mother to go through that kind of pain, he must be either too weak, too young, or a combination of both to offer any assistance. The third interesting item to note here is the manner in which she addresses Elijah, namely as a representative of the Lord God (**1 Kings 17:12**). However, just because she recognized him as a servant of the Lord doesn't mean that she's already a believer. She simply recognized an Israelite and was familiar with their God, much as Elijah was familiar with Baal.

Now we can see why the dilemma of this widow is such an interesting study. She was an ordinary woman, scraped to the bare essentials by the cruel blades of reality. There was no food, no hope for life or happiness, and no hope for the future of her young son. And yet she still fulfilled Elijah's request, which we will soon read. Here's a valuable lesson for us as well. We don't usually offer our services to another when we assume there is nothing left to give. Think about the last time you were involved in a car accident or any kind of serious collision. Were you immediately worried about the other people involved in the mishap? Or were you more concerned about yourself and your own possessions? As difficult as it is to admit, our minds usually move to assess *our* damages first, even if the other person has damages of his own. However, Jesus clearly states that we are to love our neighbors as we love ourselves. This is how He answered the Pharisees as to which are the most important commandments. **"'Love the Lord your God with all your heart and with all**

your soul and with all your mind.' This is the first and greatest commandment. And the second is like it: 'Love your neighbor as yourself.' All the Law and the Prophets hang on these two commandments." (Matthew 22:37-40). The widow, without even a good reason to do so, showed great love toward her neighbor.

Surely the widow wasn't thinking about these words as she rushed to prepare her last bit of food for Elijah. She probably didn't even know the Ten Commandments. It's far more likely that she heard the authority of the Lord in Elijah's next words. **"Don't be afraid. Go home and do as you have said. But first make a small cake of bread for me from what you have and bring it to me, and then make something for yourself and your son. For this is what the LORD, the God of Israel, says: 'The jar of flour will not be used up and the jug of oil will not run dry until the day the LORD gives rain on the land'"** (1 Kings 17:13-14). Trusting in the confident message of this bold prophet, the widow gave everything she had to a stranger in need.

The widow's blind faith would be her ultimate success. Hollywood loves to make movies about people who offer a small act of kindness to someone in need, only to find that their kindness is rewarded in large quantities. While Hollywood certainly has good intentions for showing the best in people, this scenario usually doesn't play out in real life. When you sacrifice a part of yourself for someone else, you often don't get anything in return, except perhaps a feeling of satisfaction. What satisfaction could there be in starving to death? However, the widow's actions were motivated by a need for something far greater than a full stomach. She was beginning to believe in the God of Elijah, simply through the authority of His message. Her blind faith would lead to much more than just a mouthful of bread.

"She went away and did as Elijah had told her. So there was food every day for Elijah and for the woman

and her family. For the jar of flour was not used up and the jug of oil did not run dry, in keeping with the word of the LORD spoken by Elijah" (1 Kings 17:15-16).   The widow and her son were now well fed, as was Elijah, who brought this blessing to them in the name of the Lord. What greater proof could she need to become a full believer in the Lord?

Do Old Testament-type miracles happen even today? Sure they do! Every time a baby is born, every time it rains, every time the world blooms in the spring, a miracle takes place. (**Job 37:15**). We shouldn't worry about classifying what is and isn't a miracle, just as we shouldn't try to figure out how God performs these miracles in the Bible. The important thing isn't how it happened, but *why*, and to what result. The widow is a recipient of more than one miracle, and never does she bother with the *how*, but only with the *why*.

Elijah would bring even more miracles to the house of this ordinary widow. Just when things were looking up for the woman and her son, tragedy again struck. **"Some time later the son of the woman [the widow] who owned the house became ill. He grew worse and worse, and finally stopped breathing. She said to Elijah, 'What do you have against me, man of God? Did you come to remind me of my sin and kill my son?'"** (1 Kings 17:17-18). This pagan, who had nearly died outside of the faith, finally realized her sinfulness! This was an incredible moment. She recognized not only that she had been wrong to follow a false god, but also that her pagan worship could potentially have been the reason for her son's death. She now sought Elijah's help, because she recognized God's power within him. Elijah cried out to the Lord on behalf of the widow's son, but to what avail? Would the One True God, who is ultimately Jesus Christ, the same Father, Son, and Holy Spirit (also referred to as the Holy Trinity) of the New Testament and of all time, raise this child from the dead? Absolutely!

"The LORD heard Elijah's cry, and the boy's life returned to him, and he lived. Elijah picked up the child and carried him down from the room into the house. He gave him to his mother and said, 'Look, your son is alive!'" (1 Kings 17:22-23). This miracle isn't even the most startling part of the widow's story. The Lord has the power to give life and to take it away, but that's not the primary focus of Elijah – or God. A human life, fragile and tender, can be easily snuffed out by any number of means, but the soul and eternal life of a person is what really matters. Is the widow going to believe in the God who saved her and her son from earthly death? Will she, by the grace of God, seek refuge from *eternal* death?

"Then the woman said to Elijah, 'Now I know that you are a man of God and that the word of the LORD from your mouth is the truth'" (1 Kings 17:24). You may wonder why the widow hadn't already arrived at this conclusion after the miracle of the flour and oil awhile back, but consider her circumstances. This is an ordinary widow who sees everyone she loves and trusts worshipping Baal, a false god. She knows that belief in the One True God doesn't hold much appeal or credibility in her area. She would have to become an outcast to believe in and worship this God. It's hard to make that kind of definitive life change. After all, this is no feeble old woman. The widow is a young mother with a son to care for. She now has the opportunity to spread the message of the real God to everyone she meets for the rest of her life. She may also face persecution or even death for her beliefs, but she is making that stand anyway. I'm sure that some of us have delayed making a real commitment to that in which we believe, because we are worried about potential ridicule or chastisement from our friends or family. Christ's love for us, however, is unending and immeasurable. The

Holy Spirit enlightens and sanctifies our hearts so that we have the boldness and confidence to proclaim the name of God in spite of the hardships of this world.

God calls all sorts of people to belief, and not everyone who receives His message is what we might think of as a "typical" Christian. Note the words of Jesus as He preached to His own hometown concerning His ministry and position as the Son of God. **"I assure you that there were many widows [who were believers] in Israel in Elijah's time, when the sky was shut for three and a half years and there was a severe famine throughout the land. Yet Elijah was not sent to any of them, but to a widow in Zarephath [an unbeliever] in the region of Sidon"** (Luke 4:25-26). This shows that God works through many types of people, and not all of them are what the world would consider "typical" Christians. When we proclaim the message of the Bible to others, even when we feel ordinary and incapable of such a high honor, we are doing the extraordinary work of God. This may even come when we are at the end of our rope and nothing seems right with the world. Remember this amazing story of the widow, and see that God's love has no boundaries of race, nationality, or economy. He will provide for us in all situations, regardless of our circumstances.

Study Questions

Q1. Have you ever felt so utterly divided by your various obligations that you couldn't give one more piece of yourself to anyone? Read **1 Corinthians 10:13**. Can we find hope, even in the midst of panic and overload?

Q2. See page 124. Why was Zarephath such an unlikely place for the prophet Elijah to seek refuge?

Q3. What do Christ's words in **Matthew 22:37-40** mean for us in our daily lives? What did they mean to the widow of Zarephath? Read **Galatians 5:14**. How important is it for us to love and care for our neighbor? How is this accomplished?

Q4. I speak about miracles on page 128. When discussing miracles, is it better to focus on the "how" or the "why"? Read **John 10:38** and **Hebrews 2:3-4**. Do miracles still happen today?

Q5. The widow of Zarephath, once a pagan from a pagan nation, receives the God of Israel as her own during Elijah's stay. Read **1 Kings 17:17-18**. What is our first inclination that this widow is beginning to understand the God of Israel? Read also **Romans 7:7**.

Q6. The widow of Zarephath was an unlikely candidate to share God's grace with others, but she was chosen to do so nonetheless, despite the fact that there were many other, more qualified candidates (**Luke 4:25-26**). How does God use all people to accomplish His will and all believers to share His Word? Read **Hebrews 4:12, 2 Timothy 3:16**, and **2 Corinthians 4:6-7**. Does the Word of God need our help to accomplish its means?

Joseph

¹⁸ This is how the birth of Jesus Christ came about: His mother Mary was pledged to be married to Joseph, but before they came together, she was found to be with child through the Holy Spirit. ¹⁹ Because Joseph her husband was a righteous man and did not want to expose her to public disgrace, he had in mind to divorce her quietly. (Matthew 1:18-19)

Have you ever been thrust into a spotlight that you neither wanted nor expected? What if your sudden fame was accompanied by infamy and great danger? It's kind of like winning the jackpot in the lottery. Anyone would think that all of that money will automatically bring them happiness, but what usually happens? Often, fear and isolation seize these "lucky" few until they wish they had never received this windfall in the first place. How does that apply to Joseph? He didn't buy a lottery ticket, hoping to win a million dollars. He wasn't looking for notoriety or fame. He was, however, thrust into the spotlight, only to find himself an enemy of the state and a fugitive from the law.

You know Joseph as the father of Jesus, who is the Christ. But he isn't really Jesus' father, is he? He didn't have sexual relations with the Virgin Mary prior to the birth of Jesus, so he's more of a stepfather. Joseph took his role as stepfather very seriously, risking his own life, reputation, and happiness so that Jesus and Mary might have a chance at happiness of their own. For these reasons alone, it's essential that we take a closer look at the extraordinary actions of this humble carpenter from Bethlehem.

Thanks to the genealogy at the beginning of the New Testament in the book of Matthew, we can see that Joseph is an ordinary carpenter with an extraordinary bloodline. His living is a simple and honest one, just enough to support him and his family with no extravagances. He descends, however, from such figures as Abraham, Isaac, Jacob, Rahab, Ruth, King David, and King Solomon. Joseph *had* to come from such a lineage, for it was prophesied that Jesus Christ would descend from kings: **"For to us a child is born, to us a son is given, and the government will be on his shoulders. And he will be called Wonderful Counselor, Mighty God, Everlasting Father, Prince of Peace. Of the increase of his government and peace there will be no end. He will reign on David's throne and over his kingdom, establishing and upholding it with justice and righteousness from that time on and forever. The zeal of the LORD Almighty will accomplish this"** (Isaiah 9:6-7).

While all of the Gospels (Matthew, Mark, Luke, and John) give a slightly different viewpoint of Jesus' birth and life growing up, Matthew provides us with the most detailed account of Joseph's involvement. He was pledged to be wed to a girl named Mary. This union was similar to a modern day engagement, but even more serious. *"Engagement in ancient Judaism was legally binding and required divorce if it were to be broken, but sexual relations and living together under one roof were not permitted until after the marriage ceremony."[7]* When Mary turned up pregnant with Jesus (not due to relations with Joseph), she would have been accused of a heinous crime against her husband. The Bible states very clearly that they weren't intimate before Mary got pregnant, which is vital to the rest of the story. Jesus was, after all, prophesied to be born of a virgin (**Isaiah 7:14**). Nothing else

[7] Blomberg, Craig. Vol. 22, *Matthew*. electronic ed. Logos Library System; The New American Commentary (p. 57). Nashville: Broadman & Holman, 2001, c1992.

would have sufficed. So how did Mary and Joseph maintain their social respectability and honor? Perhaps their example could inspire a generation that has lost much of its will for propriety and fidelity in committed relationships.

In today's society, sex has become a casual and sup-posedly natural right of passage for young people. Children as young as preteens are experimenting with such activities, not caring about the consequences of their actions. Equally distressing is when unmarried adults consensually have "casual" sex and completely ignore what will happen if the woman gets pregnant. If she does, the couple is thrown into a situation demanding responsibility and life-altering change that many are simply unprepared for.

Several "trash television" shows boost their ratings by bringing dysfunctional couples on the set, only to reveal to the man that he is not really the biological father of the woman's baby. Such programs characterize a common reality in our society: many people, married or unmarried, sleep around behind their partner's back. For many people, monogamy and commitment seem to be optional. This wasn't the reality in the time of Joseph and Mary. There was only one solution for Mary's apparent infidelity: she would become an outcast in her society.

According to Levitical law (**Leviticus 18:29-30**), anyone engaging in adulterous sexual relations – that is, anything outside of marriage – was to be separated from the people. They were no longer fit to be a part of the community. That person would be forced to wander to another village, hoping to be taken in. It was quite likely, however, that he or she would die from abandonment. This was the judgment facing Mary, and this was the burden on the shoulders of an honest carpenter. Joseph, however, was an honorable man who didn't want to see any harm come to Mary. **"Because Joseph her husband was a righteous man and did not want to expose her to public disgrace, he had**

in mind to divorce her quietly" (Matthew 1:19). Joseph, even before knowing that Mary's pregnancy was legitimate, decides to spare her from unnecessary shame. This is an extraordinarily decent thing to do, much like a stepfather who takes responsibility and cares for a woman and her children after the biological father has ran out on them. However, Mary and Joseph would never get that divorce.

"But after he had considered this [divorce], an angel of the Lord appeared to him in a dream and said, 'Joseph son of David, do not be afraid to take Mary home as your wife, because what is conceived in her is from the Holy Spirit. She will give birth to a son, and you are to give him the name Jesus, because he will save his people from their sins'" (Matthew 1:20-21). Now Joseph is irrevocably bound to this woman and her Son. He must accept this divine message and commit himself to this Child. Jesus (which literally means "the Lord saves") was under Joseph's fatherly care until the time when He would begin His ministry some thirty years later. We won't go into great detail here about the Christ Child's conception. It is simply enough to say that the Holy Spirit is the Father and that Mary is the mother. This is the only miraculous birth of this nature that will ever happen. This is the only Child that will ever need to be born this way. This is God come to earth to live among men as a Man. This is Jesus Christ. Joseph the carpenter has now become the stepfather and guardian to God Almighty.

Joseph doesn't dismiss the dream, but takes action. **"When Joseph woke up, he did what the angel of the Lord had commanded him and took Mary home as his wife. But he had no union with her until she gave birth to a son. And he gave him the name Jesus"** (Matthew 1:24-25). For the rest of Jesus' life, everyone He met would associate Him with this ordinary carpenter from Bethlehem, but not in a positive way: **"'Where did this Man [Jesus] get this**

wisdom and these miraculous powers?' they asked. 'Isn't this the carpenter's Son...And they took offense at Him'" (Matthew 13:54-56). Many doubted that Jesus could really be God, because they knew Him as the Son of Joseph. This was how it needed to be. How can anyone *truly* have faith in something they can already see with their own eyes? Joseph was the brilliant camouflage that kept people from seeing the Divinity in Jesus, requiring them to have faith in His message of salvation and His numerous miracles.

Christians encounter this as well. The world tells us that we're not genuine Christians if we fall from the perceived veneer of holiness that they expect to see. We're called hypocrites when the pressures of life burden us and we slip into sinful patterns. These same antagonists fail to understand that we war against our sinfulness daily and are completely dependent upon Christ for our salvation. Just as Jesus' divinity was "hidden" behind the ordinary nature of His parents, so also the Holy Spirit who resides in all Christians is "hidden" behind our sinful nature. Philip and the other disciples had difficulty believing that Jesus is God, even going so far as to say to Him: **"Lord, show us the Father and that will be enough for us"** (John 14:8). What Christ knew, and what we must come to know, is that God works through His Word – period. Despite what others cannot or simply refuse to see, all Christians are saved children of God through the death and resurrection of Jesus Christ!

Joseph's troubles weren't over yet. To understand the following events, a little background must be provided. Jesus was being hailed as the Messiah, or Savior, from His very birth. This upset and worried the current ruler, Herod, so much that he plotted to have this Child killed before He could take over the throne. How could Herod do such a thing? He was the kind of guy who killed his own family to be ruler, so why not kill this obscure Child of a carpenter? Once

Bethlehem was crawling with Herod's troops, Joseph and Mary were forced to flee to another area or risk the death of Jesus and perhaps even the loss of their own lives.

"An angel of the Lord appeared to Joseph in a dream. 'Get up,' he said, 'take the child and his mother and escape to Egypt. Stay there until I tell you, for Herod is going to search for the child to kill him'" (Matthew 2:13). Again Joseph receives a vision, but this time there is no comfort in the message – only fear. Now he and his family had to leave their home and everything familiar to hide out in Egypt, a land of foreigners. **"So he got up, took the child and his mother during the night and left for Egypt, where he stayed until the death of Herod"** (Matthew 2:14-15a). Here we see another example of Joseph's extraordinary faith. He didn't hesitate to act on the divine message, but instead gathered his family and belongings and fled to Egypt, just as he was instructed. This wasn't some weekend trip to the Holiday Inn, either. They had to remain in exile – far outside of Herod's jurisdiction – until the king's death, however long that might be. There is no doubt that in fleeing to Egypt, Joseph saved his Son's life. Herod, in his anger, killed all the babies that were approximately Jesus' age in Bethlehem and the surrounding area in an effort to ensure the infant Messiah's death. This event will forever be referred to as the "slaughter of the holy innocents."

Does this sort of "fight or flight" scenario occur in our own lives? In this situation, staying and fighting would have been foolish – and the consequences deadly. The only reasonable option was to run away. Sometimes we choose to fight battles that shouldn't ever be fought. The world tells us that it's romantic and courageous to stand against every bad thing in this world, using force whenever necessary. While this "battle to the death" mentality provides many successful movie plots for Hollywood blockbusters, it seldom bodes well for anyone in the real world. Why do we find it so shameful to seek help from others or to flee from harm? In the case of Joseph and Mary, standing their ground and fighting was the opposite of what God instructed. Sometimes fleeing a harmful situation is the right thing to do, and the only sensible solution.

Joseph received one more dream concerning his Son, which instructed him to come home after the death of Herod. On their way home, however, the Angel suddenly warned them *again* against returning. Archelaus was now ruling, and his reign would be no less treacherous than that of his father. **"Having been warned in a dream, he [Joseph (and his family)] withdrew to the district of Galilee, and he went and lived in a town called Nazareth. So was fulfilled what was said through the prophets: 'He [Jesus] will be called a Nazarene'"** (Matthew 2:22-23). At last, Joseph and his family have found a home. From this point on, until the time of His eventual death on the cross, this Son of an ordinary carpenter will be referred to as Jesus of Nazareth.

What kind of impression do we leave on our children? Jesus probably wasn't a difficult child to raise; after all, He never sinned. The pressure, however, of raising the future Savior of the world would have been immense. So great was the task that Mary has been wrongly heralded by the Roman Catholic Church as more than a mortal, even sinless. It is interesting to note, though, that Joseph is rarely (if ever) considered to have been without sin. He also played a very limited role in the story of Jesus that we have from the Gospels. We get the sense that he realized and embraced his role as a stepfather. There is no doubt that he was involved in his Son's life: Jesus Himself became a carpenter, a tribute to the work of His earthly father figure.

Joseph and others like him are some of the greatest heroes of the Bible. These are the quiet and ordinary support characters that do their duty and live upright lives so that those around them are capable of extraordinary things. God works through them every bit as much as those who have had entire books of the Bible devoted to them. Joseph will always be known for his role in the upbringing of Jesus, but he is a man worthy of special acknowledgment in his own right. This humble carpenter made sure that God's will was done on earth through His Son, Jesus Christ. Jesus' ultimate work on the cross and in His ministry can be attributed, in part, to the love and mercy that Joseph demonstrated, which was a reflection of a greater love – the love of God.

Study Questions

Q1. Have you ever wanted to win the lottery? In what ways do you think your life would change? See page 133. How was Joseph's life like winning the lottery?

Q2. See pages 135-136. How are Joseph's honorable actions toward Mary quite extraordinary, especially in light of today's culture? Read **Leviticus 18:29** and **20:10**. What would have happened to Mary if he had blown the whistle on her pregnancy?

Q3. Nativity scenes are a staple in almost every Christian household and church lawn in December. Our hearts are lifted and warmed by remembering the birth of our Savior. Read **Matthew 2:13-18**. Despite the beauty and tranquility of a nativity scene, does it adequately portray the emotions and activities of the first Christmas? How is the reality of the world different from the peaceful glimpse offered by a warm and fuzzy nativity scene?

Q4. Read **Matthew 13:53-57** and **Mark 6:1-6**. How did people use Joseph and his station in life against Jesus? See also pages 136-137. How might our circumstances or attributes act as camouflage for God's Word? How might they aid in spreading God's Word?

Q5. Love is great. We love to be loved and we love loving others (whew!). How did Joseph show his love for Jesus and Mary? How did Joseph, or any of us, learn how to love in the first place? Read **John 3:16** and **15:13**. How does God show us that He loves us?

Epilogue

Which character did you learn the most from? Perhaps you're similar to Jonah, always running away from commitments, despite the numerous talents with which you've been gifted. Even when things are going your way, you still manage to find the negative in a situation. Maybe like Solomon, you take the wealth that has been laid before you and squander it on the frivolities and pleasures of this life. Hopefully, as with Solomon, you'll soon realize that all earthly pleasures are fleeting. Long after the excitement has faded, one is left feeling hollow and vulnerable to the evils of this world. Many of us are like Nicodemus, hearing the clear message of salvation from the mouth of our Savior, but misinterpreting this truth and hesitating to act upon it. A few might even associate themselves with the widow from Zarephath. She witnessed many miracles from the prophet Elijah, but only the death of her son – and his subsequent healing – could open her eyes to God's glory. Do you find yourself identifying with any of these characters? If so, that makes you extremely normal! There's nothing more common in this world than those who seek their own pleasure with limited human understanding, only to find that no lasting comfort can be found in earthly indulgences.

Hopefully, all of us will feel a very positive and uplifting connection to someone in this book. Maybe you're a Ruth, always staying true to the ones who need you the most, even in the face of potential hardship and struggle. Fear not, for your reward will be great in heaven: **"Do not store up for yourselves treasures on earth, where moth and rust destroy, and where thieves break in and steal. But store up for yourselves treasures in heaven, where moth and rust do not destroy, and where thieves do not**

break in and steal. For where your treasure is, there your heart will be also" (Matthew 6:19-21). This treasure can never be taken away. Maybe you or somebody you know has dealt with a situation like Esther's. She was plunged into a position of power and authority, only to make a necessary stand and risk losing it all for the benefit of her people. Sometimes making the right decision can mean choosing between doing what is right and what is easy. As we reflect upon how things ended up for Esther, we realize that a truly wise person seeks the good of many. Joseph certainly did. He made it his life's goal to see that God's Son reached adulthood and accomplished His mission of salvation on the cross. Perhaps you've been unsuccessful in seeking the Lord, and have never found the satisfaction that you thought you deserved. Look to Zacchaeus, and realize that no matter how hard we search, we'll only know the Lord when He comes to us and calls us by our name: **"God, who has called you into fellowship with his Son Jesus Christ our Lord, is faithful"** (1 Corinthians 1:9).

When we, the lost sheep of the Good Shepherd Jesus Christ (**John 10:11-16**), are found and brought back home, it's a cause for celebration. When this occurs for you, don't ignore the newfound passion ignited in your heart. Lydia certainly didn't, taking her newfound faith and helping to build one of the first churches. Hanna similarly clung to her faith and was generously rewarded in the end. We also mustn't forget Elisha, who was whisked away from the comfortable routine of farming into a life of profound service and miraculous events as God's prophet. Perhaps your reception of faith will at first appear selfish, such as with Rahab, who sought her family's safety from the coming destruction. Remember that all who see the Lord through the eyes of faith will receive the same reward, namely eternal life. Rahab, despite her many and various shortcomings, is more celebrated than faithful Lydia, even holding the honor as one of Jesus' ancestors! Remember that God is the *only* one who sees our faith into completion and holds it until the very end: **"He who began a good work in you will carry it on to completion until the day of Christ Jesus"** (Philippians 1:6).

Almost any character throughout the entire Bible would be appropriate for this book. If I had chosen to use King David, Abraham the Patriarch, or even the apostle Paul, I would have written the same things with only a slightly different context. They, too, were ordinary people who accomplished the extraordinary when God worked in their lives. Look for these powerful servants, as well as many others, in my second volume, *More Extraordinary News for Ordinary People: Biblical Giants of Faith*, as we continue to explore God's extraordinary grace in our lives. We are all ordinary sinners in need of grace, and even the biggest names in the Bible experienced their share of failure and dejection.

By God's grace, David was transformed from a lowly shepherd boy into one of the greatest kings in the history of the world. However, given all that he had, David still spilled much blood, as well as engaged in an adulterous relationship, which hurt his status in the eyes of the Lord. Abraham was so well-revered that he had the distinction of being known as "God's friend." He frequently spoke with the Lord and is commended throughout the Bible for his faith and obedience. Even this didn't stop him from lying, doubting, and becoming the husband of more than one wife. Paul, who has been credited as the author of 13 books in the New Testament, began his life as Saul, a Pharisee and persecutor of Christians. He was clueless until God knocked him on his backside and made him see the light. We're all guilty of shortcomings, and these faults could eat us alive if we truly felt a need to be perfect. The Bible tells us that we aren't perfect, and never will be: **"All have sinned and fall short of the glory of God"** (Romans 3:23). These Biblical characters, with all of their weaknesses, still have something in common – or rather some*one*, to be more specific: Jesus Christ.

Jesus is the Good Shepherd: **"I am the good shepherd...I lay down my life for the sheep"** (John 10:14-15). He is ever vigilant to His flock, and He will carefully search for any lamb that strays or gets lost: **"If a man owns a hundred sheep, and one of them wanders away, will he not leave the ninety-nine on the hills and go to look for the one that wandered off... In the same way your Father in heaven is not willing that any of these little ones should be lost"** (Matthew 18:12,14). For all of the lost sheep of the world, I write this book. I hope that once you've read it, you can share it with a friend. The message of Christ crucified is simple, but it's the most profound truth that we will ever hear in this life. Recognizing Christ's great sacrifice and love for you may seem like an easy task, but it makes all the difference in the world. Seek the cross, and you'll find your salvation. This is *the* extraordinary news for all of us wonderfully ordinary people!

ANSWERS AND COMMENTARY

Jonah

1. Jonah is someone we may easily relate to, because he reacts very much like we might. He knows that Nineveh is a sinful nation, deserving of God's wrath. He doesn't want them to repent and be saved. He wants them to get what is coming to them (**4:1-2**)! He is not placing his trust in God's mercy and discernment. We do the same when we insist on dictating our own course of events throughout our lives. Everything is fine until we are presented with a "road block" that makes life difficult and shoves us out of our comfort zones. When we look back at these hard times, however, we often find that these are the moments which strengthen an already powerful relationship with our heavenly Father.

2. God commanded Jonah's attention with a storm so grand that it had the weathered fishermen on Jonah's boat fearing for their lives. After many failed attempts to calm the storm, they eventually appeal to Jonah, who by this point had understood God's message all too well. He gives a straightforward and solid declaration of his faith in **verse 9** and even prescribes the solution in **verse 12**. Jonah gets it. Through his bold testimony, along with a terror of this God who commands the sea and the waves (**Psalm 89:9**), even the pagan fishermen come to faith in the One True God (**verse 16**). Paul clearly explains this phenomenon in **2 Corinthians 12:7-10**, where He states that God places these "thorns in our flesh" to drive us to the power and comfort of Christ instead of trusting in our own strength.

3. Jonah did understand God's message on the boat. How-
    ever, it's likely at this point that he still had no intentions
    of preaching to Nineveh, and God would not allow him to
    shirk this responsibility. After spending three days and
    nights inside of a stinky, cramped fish belly, Jonah was
    finally beginning to understand that he couldn't avoid the
    tasks set before him. The admission that he makes in the
    second chapter, especially **verses 8-9**, shows a new man.
    God worked this change in Jonah and now he is ready to
    preach to Nineveh. According to **Hebrews 12**, God was
    disciplining Jonah as a child. We follow this pattern with
    our own children as well. Children need discipline to
    grow in their faith and ability to respond with love and
    compassion to an unloving and uncompassionate world.
    Children hate the discipline while it's happening, of
    course, because it's unpleasant. We all have experienced
    this, either in our lives as children or as parents.
    However, those of us who have grown and benefited from
    the discipline will eventually appreciate our parents for
    doing what they could to imitate God's love in this way.

    Beyond teaching Jonah a lesson, God is showing
    His gracious and compassionate nature. He could have
    simply abandoned Jonah and found someone else to
    complete the task. However, He chose to work with
    Jonah so that this reluctant prophet would learn from this
    situation. All those who would still doubt God's
    compassion can think of it this way: there are two ways
    out of a fish's belly. God chose the preferable exit
    strategy (being spit out), even when Jonah deserved the
    other (use your imagination)!

4. Repentance makes for a difficult subject matter. The
    book of Jonah, however, provides an excellent framework
    for explanation. Only after God brought Jonah to the
    depths of despair could he truly repent of his

unwillingness and obstinate refusal of God's will. Only through the preaching of God Word (through Jonah) can the Ninevites come to repent of their sins and receive God's salvation.

Paul speaks to those who mistakenly feel that repentance is something that they themselves can accomplish in **Romans 2**, where he states that only God's kindness (undeserved love through Jesus Christ) can bring true repentance. Being repentant does not mean that you cease to sin. On the contrary, we all sin every moment of our lives. Repentance, however, worked through faith, reminds us that we are sinful and continually drives us back into the arms of Christ, our faithful Shepherd, who redeemed us from our sin.

5. Jonah is deeply depressed and asks God to let him die. Why such a dramatic reaction? Jonah is angry because the sinful Ninevites were so quick to repent and God was so good to them. He is wondering why they get all of the good treatment while he gets ordered around like some sort of slave. Veteran Christians sometimes feel this way about new converts as well. We see how over-the-top excited they are (as they have every right to be) when they first come to faith and we get jealous of their zeal. Those who have been "in the trenches" of Christianity for decades, faithfully serving, will be less likely to bubble at the name of Jesus, but what replaces this excitement is something even greater. Solid, unwavering faith is the result of a lifetime in the Lord. Obviously Jonah still doesn't get it.

6. Poor Jonah. He gets thrown from a boat, swallowed by a fish, is forced to preach to a quarter million dirty sinners (who repent), and what does he get? Jonah is upset because he feels like a conscripted laborer. He's upset

because Nineveh wasn't destroyed.   Isn't that terribly ordinary of him?   God then gives him a vine to ease his suffering, and now he's the picture of smug satisfaction as he awaits God's judgment upon Nineveh.   You can almost hear his thoughts: "I have a vine given to me from God Himself.   He must really appreciate my work to give me such a wonderful gift."

God then destroys the vine and sends hot winds to teach Jonah yet another lesson.   You see, Jonah doesn't care about the people of Nineveh.   He'd just as soon see them burn.   However, he became very attached to his fancy vine, and was understandably upset at it being destroyed.   God, in His divine wisdom, points out to Jonah that the vine is insignificant, but that Nineveh is considerable.   Shouldn't God care about Nineveh much more than Jonah cares about his vine?   Ahhh, now Jonah gets it.   There is more to this world that his own desires.

We often wonder why God allows difficult and painful events to happen in our lives.   They don't seem at all pleasant at the time.   However, when we look back and see what God was doing, we can see that He touches many lives through our suffering as well as our joy.   What a revelation it is to discover that there is more to this life than our own selfish wants and desires!

Lydia

1. Lydia faced many risks for being open with her faith. We know that she was open with her faith because she was present with the others who came to listen to Paul preach. By including herself in such company, she was risking her livelihood, her friends, and even her family. Everything she had worked so hard to build might be snatched away in an instant by disapproving Romans who weren't keen on the idea of this new "cult," Christianity.

    We, too, face risks because of our faith even today. I was once a library clerk in my hometown. I used to finish my e-mails with "God's Blessings," which was the most natural thing for me to say. I was informed, after a few weeks of using this phrase, that I was prohibited from mentioning God in my e-mails, lest I offend someone. I was just a library clerk. Imagine if my entire living (and in Lydia's case, a substantial living) depended on my willingness to ignore my faith at work! How many God-fearing people are too timid to express their faith publicly?

    Jesus clearly states in **Matthew 10** that the life of a believer is harder than that of the unbeliever. This is because our true enemies (the Devil, the world, and our own sinful nature) will attack us much harder when we depend on God for our comfort, rather than on the things of this world. Why would Satan care about those whom he has already separated from God's love? His target is baptized Christians. When Christians recognize and understand that their lives will be harder because of the Cross, but still remain firm in their faith, this is called a "Theology of the Cross." Imagining that life should be much easier for Christians, and that God will simply give you what you want because you have enough faith in

Christ, is called a "Theology of Glory." Stay away from this mindset, lest the devil should lead you to despair. Read **1 Peter 4:12-16**. For further exploration of this concept, I direct your attention also to *On Being a Theologian of the Cross* by Gerhard Forde, which is a concise and modern exploration of Luther's *Heidelberg Disputation* of 1518.

2. While Judaism may have been the closest religion to Christianity, they were not one and the same. Many Jews, who were part of a recognized religion at the time, persecuted the newly formed and often misunderstood Christian church. Despite this, however, Lydia came to believe in this message of Christ crucified that Paul was preaching (**1 Corinthians 1:23**). Many people want to take credit for their own conversion. Christianity is absolutely torn on this issue. Many Christians believe that a person must "make a decision for Christ" in order to be truly saved. This text, however, clearly states that **"the Lord opened Lydia's heart to Paul's message"** (Acts 16:14). The apostle Peter also uses this language when describing God's mission to the Gentiles just a chapter earlier (**Acts 15:8-9**). God comes to *us*, not the other way around. He comes to us through His Holy Word, which even here did not return empty. Lydia came to faith through Paul's preaching of God's Word! However, the best was yet to come.

3. Baptism is God's work for us. It is not our work for God. As is clearly evidenced in this passage, Lydia did come to faith before her baptism. This is because God's Word can and will affect faith even without the miracle of baptism (**Romans 10:17**). However, as we read in **Mark 16:16** and **Titus 3:4-8**, God works through baptism, when connected with His Word, to produce faith in us. How

important is this? It's just about the most important thing of all. This means that we baptize infants, even those who cannot "make a decision" at all. In the case of baptism, it is always God that makes the decision for us. Lydia believes this as well, and she has her whole family, children included, baptized. We don't read that her family members were all faithful Christians prior to their baptisms. It's likely that they weren't. However, the gift of baptism has the power to work that faith in them! That is why Paul openly baptized these "unbelievers" into the Christian faith. This also happens in the very next section with the jailer at Philippi (**Acts 16:29-33**).

4. Lydia didn't simply thank Paul and his companions and send them on their way. Because of her faith, she was moved to *show* them that she had experienced a change of heart by the grace of God (**Luke 6:43-45**). She invited the men into her home, where they could rest their weary bodies and obtain some comfort in the midst of their journey. By the Bible's mere mention that she challenges them to test the authenticity of her conversion and that she "persuaded" them, we get the idea that she's working pretty hard to get them to accept her invitation. Paul, not to mention the others, was extremely driven and dedicated to his task. To take any time away from his missionary journey was significant, but even he eventually acquiesced to her kindness.

   Likewise, our lives can never be the same once we become Christians. We still sin constantly, and we are daily reminded of our sinful flesh, but we also know that we are redeemed in Christ. In light of this status as God's forgiven children, we live sanctified lives for our friends and neighbors. *Sanctified* is an important word. It means to grow in divine grace as a result of baptism and conversion. It's the natural process of God's redeemed.

Lydia was drawn, by the Spirit of God, to do this as well. God's love and grace is then spread through our lives as well as the faithful saints of the past. Glory be to God that He can work such faith and good works in the lives of even wretched sinners like us! Read **Ephesians 2:8-10**.

5. Lydia, the successful business woman, had now turned her house into a church and meeting place for God's faithful to convene and worship as they wished. She had certainly come a long way in her spiritual growth, but we don't hear that she gave up her day job. Lydia didn't simply become a full time church worker because she was a redeemed Christian. She saw that her own vocation and place in life was ideally suited for service in God's kingdom. For one thing, selling purple goods was a very profitable enterprise. Through this business, she could afford to make her house a place of meeting, and provide other financial assistance as well. God never intended for everyone in the Bible to become an apostle. In fact, He made it very clear that only some were selected to be overseers (**1 Timothy 3**). Never fear, for there's plenty of work left for the rest of us!

If everyone were a church worker or pastor, how would the church ever survive? How would we eat if there were no farmers? Where would we live if there were no carpenters? Jesus remained a carpenter until the three years before His death. Paul remained a tent maker throughout his ministry. We can all serve God in whatever job we are currently employed. If you make a good salary, as is the case with Lydia, you can offer financial assistance to benefit the Kingdom. If you are a carpenter or farmer, you can lend your expertise to the church. Even simply telling your co-workers and friends about the joy that you have in Christ (**1 Peter 3:15**) is an excellent way in which God will work through your position in life.

You may operate a cash register. You may drive a bus. You may be a "dealer of purple." Whatever your role in life, God will use your unique talents and abilities to further His kingdom.

Elisha

1. God accomplishes many things through this succession. Elijah had developed quite a following through the miracles that God allowed him to accomplish. So many were his great deeds, in fact, that he was in danger of being worshiped himself. This would not do. When Elisha took over as God's number one prophet, it became clear that God was working these extraordinary miracles, not men. Elijah had to move on. He had done all that he could in his current position. There was no more work for him. There was, however, much for Elisha still to accomplish. This is God's way.

    We see this pattern today with modern pastors, albeit slightly modified. A pastor only stays in one place until he feels it's time for another ordinary man to step in and carry on God's work. One pastor may be completely at the end of his ability to help a congregation, while another pastor may have many contributions to make. Although the pastor doesn't get to pick who follows him in leading the congregation, the next man is most certainly his successor. The key here is that it is God, not the pastor, who works faith in our hearts and performs miraculous wonders each and every day!

2. The purpose of the prophets was to keep bringing God's rebellious people back to the truth. God's people were constantly straying from His truth, worshiping idols, and turning their backs on Him. The prophets, by contrast, spoke nothing but God's truth, and much of it is recorded in the Bible. We have just as much need to hear these truths today. Often, the prophets spoke to bring people back to the laws which God handed down to Moses. This is why a series of prophets similar to Moses followed

after his death. However, as is revealed in such passages as **Hebrews 3** and **Matthew 5**, One was to come who would end this lineage and bring true peace to God's people.

That long awaited One is Jesus Christ, God's own Son, who is indeed the last of the prophets. Why is this distinction important? Muslims (and they are by no means alone in this) maintain that Jesus was a prophet, but that there were others after Him. They falsely believe that, as important as Jesus was, Mohammed came after Him and revealed much more for God's true people. The Mormons also believe in modern prophecy. This practice allows them to change God's will as they please. There are disastrous consequences for denying Christ as the last prophet. And Christ isn't just the last prophet – He is the *greatest* prophet.

As we see in **Hebrews 3**, Christ is likened to the architect, with Moses as His creation. This is certainly true. In light of this, we can hold Moses in high esteem, but only insofar as we realize that he was simply a precursor of the One who was to come, Jesus the Christ. Also, in **Matthew 5**, Jesus states His true intentions. Whereas the other prophets simply carried forth and reminded God's chosen people of the laws of Moses, Jesus actually fulfilled all aspects of this law. God's law demands perfection, which we cannot fulfill, despite our very best efforts and good intentions. Only a perfect being could accomplish this. Christ accomplished this for us. Praise be to God for the inexpressible gift that we have been given through His Son!

3. It's not difficult to see that Elisha had a pretty comfortable life. He was the son of a wealthy farmer and had inherited a lucrative lifestyle, which allowed him to live and work alongside his parents. This is not to say

that things were always easy for him, but only that he didn't need to fear or wonder about his future. Then this renowned prophet Elijah stops by and turns everything on its ear. How does Elisha respond? He drops everything and follows him.

Elisha wisely ascertains that this is God calling him to service and not only Elijah, a mere man. He dives into this new life face first. He proves his dedication to God's calling by leaving all traces of his old life behind, even destroying the last vestiges of his former success so that he wouldn't be tempted to return to this life. He was in God's hands now.

Even today we find ourselves in similar situations. A pastor never knows when he will get a call to another section of the country (or the world, for that matter). However, you need not be a clergyman to get relocated for any number of reasons. Divorce, death, a new job, and all other manner of conditions cause us to change and to alter our perceptions of life and what it has to offer. However – as I mentioned on page 44 – when we place our trust in Christ, we know that we will always be provided for, no matter how difficult life may get. And it will be difficult at times (see **Matthew 8:18-22**). But God's promise for you is that He will care for you in this life until you are called home to your final destination, heaven.

4. Elisha, working by God's hand, could have simply looked at the river, the polluted water, or the dying child. God doesn't need salt, a cloak, or a prophet lying on a child to perform His miracles. However, using these means allows us to understand better the source of the miracle being worked because we know that cloaks and salt aren't magical in themselves. One common element that does occur throughout Scripture is prayer. Prayer is powerful

and it works! Read **Philippians 4:6**. God listens to our prayers and has promised to give us all that we need. How comforting for ordinary sinners like us!

5. Naaman was a great man. As we see in **2 Kings 5**, he was the commander of the army of Aram. He was a valiant soldier and highly regarded by his people. However, he had leprosy (see page 48), and it was going to take his life. There was nothing he could do about it. However, a slave girl who had been captured from Israel would lead him to his eventual healing. By all means, she could have watched him rot until the day he died, but she didn't. She knew that there was only one way that he could be healed, and she didn't safeguard the information. She desired that he should know the wondrous God of her people and what He was capable of. Even in the midst of her suffering, she seeks to help her own captors. This isn't exactly an ordinary reaction from someone in such a lowly position. God doesn't need greatness. He can work through anyone!

This applies to us as well. God desires that every Christian share his or her faith, both in word and deed, and has equipped His church for the task. This doesn't mean that we must go around knocking on doors and handing out religious tracts. In fact, God has uniquely and perfectly positioned us in our lives so that wherever we find ourselves or whatever our situation in life, we might be ready to give an account for the hope that we have in Christ Jesus (**1 Peter 3:15**). This is certainly the case with this slave girl from Israel. God's message of truth isn't hampered by our position in life, but in fact is spread through it.

It's also notable that Naaman, after coming to an understanding of God's great power (**2 Kings 5:15, 17**), also becomes a powerful witness of God's grace. He takes his faith into Aram, where he has influence over a multitude of the king's soldiers, and others besides. He, like the Israelite girl who first directed him to Elisha, has been uniquely placed in life so that he might reach many with God's truth.

6. Naaman at first refuses because Elisha's instructions seem too ordinary. He gets angry because he expected some great event to take place prior to his cleansing. Nothing in his experience had prepared him for Elisha's command. He couldn't lower himself to wash in such a muddy puddle as the Jordan. There were many fine streams and rivers outside of Israel. Why not them? His lack of understanding seemed sufficient to refuse the gift. He had his pride, after all!

Upon returning, however, his servants proved once again how much they understood. Read **2 Kings 5:13**. Here they make a great observation about God's method. He uses very ordinary things to perform great miracles. The ordinary nature (and perhaps dirty nature) of the Jordan had initially repulsed Naaman, but now he understands the true beauty of God's way. He is cleansed and becomes a powerful witness in Aram!

This is also how Baptism and Communion are often misunderstood as well. In these Sacraments (which is another word for God's gifts with a promise attached), God combines His Word and promise with very ordinary elements. In Baptism, it's plain water. In Communion, it's wine and bread. By themselves, these things have no power (just like the Jordan River). However, when God joins His promise to them they are life-giving Sacraments that connect us with the death of Christ. This cannot be seen with the eyes, but only with eyes of faith. These same eyes of faith brought Namaan to the Jordan, where he was healed of his leprosy.

For excellent Bible passages mentioning Communion, see **Matthew 26:17-29**; **Mark 14:22-24**; **Luke 22:7-23**; and **1 Corinthians 11:17-34**. For more information concerning Baptism, see **Titus 3:5-8** and **Romans 6:3-5**.

Esther

1. Despite the many wonderful and miraculous things that happen throughout the Bible, there is only one thread that stitches together the hodge-podge of Biblical characters – trust in God.   They didn't rely solely upon their own abilities and talents, but upon the Giver, knowing that those abilities were a gift from God.

   Paul says here in Romans that everyone – Jews and Gentiles alike – will be saved if their trust is in Christ. God works this trust in us through the power of His Holy Word and His precious Sacraments of Baptism, Communion, and Absolution (the Sacrament of forgiveness).   Glory be to God for working this miracle in us!

2. Esther was wise, beautiful, and had a sweet disposition. We see in **Esther 2:9** that she immediately pleased the Eunuch that was in charge of the wedding competition. By gaining his attention and admiration, she was assuring a leading spot among the most favored of women vying for the king's affections.   It's significant to note that she didn't just brazenly enter this contest without considering her competition.   She carefully listened to the counsel of Mordecai, her cousin, and that of Hegai, the chief Eunuch.   Her strict obedience played as much a part in her eventual victory as any of her other talents.

   Esther's actions remind us of the words of Jesus many centuries later, in His sermon concerning talents and the proper use of those we are given (**Matthew 25:14-30**).   Our talents are not to be used for our own selfish gain, but for the glory of God.   Esther acted in such a way.   We see that Esther is not driven by a sense of selfishness or greed, but by a love for her people and her God.

3. Mordecai knew that bowing to an earthly ruler would be displeasing to the God of Israel, who is, by self-definition, a jealous God (**Exodus 20:5**). As noted previously, he was to bow to God alone. This may not appear to be a similar message to the one in **Romans 13**, but in fact it is. Think of it as the same message with different packaging. Paul is saying here that we must respect and listen to our governing authorities (governors, senators, presidents, even kings) as they act in God's stead. God has established such positions for earthly rulers so that we might have order in this life. He would have expected Mordecai to bow down to a just ruler as well. However, Haman was not a God-fearing man. Even today, we obey the authorities only insofar as they follow God's commands and statues, as laid out in the Bible.

   This sort of subject matter really highlights the beliefs and activities of certain cults, like the Jehovah's Witnesses, who say that they answer to no authority but God Himself. They have ignored the words of Paul, who teaches us that earthly governments are established by God. However, even as we obey the law of the land, we do ourselves harm when we attach ourselves to such laws as homosexual rights, legalized abortion, and other non-Biblical ideals. Here it is our Christian responsibility to follow God rather than men (**Acts 5:29**).

4. Mordecai's warnings are severe, but warranted. If Esther allows her people to suffer at the hand of the heathen, she will have aligned herself with the earthly power and not with the God of her people. She rightly feared God's wrath and wisely chose to help her people, who were in mortal danger. She could have easily refused Mordecai and taken the easy way out.

   Even today we find ourselves having to choose between a comfortable lifestyle and remaining true to our beliefs. We are told by society to conceal all vestiges of our faith. We are encouraged to be Christians only on Sunday, but not during the rest of the week, when we are out in the world and spending time among the heathen. This is Satan's great deception. He wants us to believe that our lives will be a living hell if we wear our Christianity outwardly. And the danger is real. As we read in **1 Peter 5:8**, our true enemy is the Devil, and he is a roaring lion just waiting to devour us. However, Christ rightly says that we truly have nothing to fear from the Devil and this world (**Luke 12:4-5**). Our enemies will assail us, but we need not fear them. Our God will protect us until the very end. Esther understood this. She risked everything in this life for her faith. This makes an ordinary person truly extraordinary!

5. Esther was a meek and mild helpmate for her husband, the great King Xerxes. As we see in **Esther 4**, she wasn't willing to disturb him, although he had been in council for a month! In **chapters 5-7**, she gently and humbly builds her request, explaining how she wishes to help her people from experiencing a most savage death. She could have stormed into the chamber, demanded that her people be saved, and depend on her lofty position as the queen. But she doesn't.

   We see in **Ephesians 5** that God has ordered a proper relationship between husband and wife to be one of give and take. Women are to subject themselves to their husbands (**5:22**). As our society strives to convince us that men and women are the same (men and women are certainly valued equally, but God made us marvelously different!), women have an increasingly difficult time seeing subjection as an ideal position. However, when men love their wives with the sacrificial love of Christ for His church (**5:25**), there should be no problem in subjection. When everything is done according to God's plan, neither side should feel the least bit compromised. And even though Esther is meek and mild, she successfully captures her husband's attention.

By using all of the skills and abilities that God had given her, Esther convinced the king that he was making a grave mistake by ordering that the Jews be killed. This is the same man who divorced his previous wife, Vashti, because she disobeyed a direct order. Esther is aware of Xerxes' temperament, and she finds a clever way to reach him *despite* it. In doing so, she demonstrates the symmetry of give and take that characterizes a Christian marriage. The result? The Jews are granted pardon and Mordecai, Esther's cousin, is given Haman's old position. In the end, God has truly exalted Esther from a queen to a savior of her people. This was His extraordinary plan from the beginning, and we marvel that He would use an ordinary woman like Esther to carry it to completion.

Ruth

1. We all know people who, at first glance, seem to live very uneventful lives – only to find out later that they have achieved some extraordinary things. In their humility, we may not have ever heard of their good deeds (at least not from them). However, their lives of faith produce a trail of change and joy that cannot be hidden. God works great things through the most unassuming people!

2. Ruth's story of tribulation reminds us of Job's. She loses her husband and finds herself without anyone to support her. Now she, along with Naomi and Orpah, will travel to Naomi's home town of Bethlehem – located in the land of Judah – seeking provisions. Her situation seems pretty bleak.

   Sometimes in our own lives we find ourselves at major crossroads. Perhaps in the wake of a spouse's death or financial bankruptcy, we wonder why God is so angry with us. We imagine that He's punishing us for something we did incorrectly. This is why Ruth's story is so important. We read in her story that God had great plans for her that could only have happened through these terrible circumstances. God has great plans for you as well! When we are in the midst of the darkness, we don't always see the light at the end of the tunnel – but it *is* there.

   The words of Paul and Peter in their respective epistles are so comforting during times of disaster and loss. We read here and elsewhere in their letters that our suffering as Christians is an honor. God is testing our faith, which is more precious than gold. God was also testing the faith of Ruth. Did she pass the test?

3. Orpah and Ruth both resist at first, but eventually the enticement of a better life (or simply the hope of survival) overcomes Orpah, and she leaves Naomi. She wanted a husband and children. She thought staying with Naomi would find her a very young widow and scrounging out an existence. Nobody wants that. Ruth, however saw beyond her material existence to the real purpose for her life. She was to be a believer in the One True God of Naomi and Elimilech. She would rather abandon all that she has known in Moab to be with Naomi – and the God of Naomi's people – in Bethlehem. This relationship was worth more to her than any number of pagan husbands and worldly treasures. She was, quite literally, storing up treasures in heaven (**Matthew 6:19-21**).

So how would we choose to respond in such a situation? We would be dishonest if we said that we'd choose to stay with Naomi every time. We sinful humans are more likely to take the easy way out. However, God's will cannot be thwarted by our shortcomings. We don't credit Ruth's faith and determination to some inner strength, but to God's grace in her life. We can be confident that God will work the same strength in us, when all we want to do is duck out the back.

4. God's plan unfolds in glorious splendor as we now see connections and reasons for things that were previously a complete mystery. All of the "whys" of Ruth's life are being answered. Why did you have me marry, only to allow my husband to die? Why did you have me move far away from my home in Moab to Bethlehem? The answer: Boaz.

Boaz has absolutely no connection to Ruth, other than her marriage and close connection to her mother-in-law. Elimelech, Naomi's deceased husband, is related to Boaz. In light of this relationship, they might find some small kindness from him. It should be noted that they weren't even looking for him in the first place. Ruth, trying to gather some grain for their survival, happens upon his field. He inquires about her and learns of her loyalty to Naomi and to God. Ruth is about to learn quite a bit concerning the character of this God-fearing man.

Boaz immediately provides much more than was expected. First he marvels at Ruth's faith and dedication to Naomi and God (**2:11-12**). Ruth wanted only to glean in his fields. After inviting her to eat with him, he allows her the choicest areas for gathering, instructs his gatherers to leave some behind for her, and prohibits anyone from doing her any harm (which they probably would have done without his warning). This is just the beginning.

5. Naomi insightfully interpreted Boaz's kind actions as budding love. She determined that he was a good man who would make a fitting husband for Ruth. The plan that she comes up with sounds odd to our western way of thinking, but it was an acceptable method in Biblical times. Ruth was to sneak onto the threshing floor, uncover Boaz's feet, and lie down next to them. This may sound sexual and deviant to our ears; however, Boaz wasn't the kind of man to fall victim to simple lusts of the flesh. The absolute confidence of Naomi, coupled with her observance of Boaz's character, leads the reader to better understand her plan and its subsequent success.

The result? Boaz is overjoyed to see Ruth offering herself to him, not sexually, but in marriage. Beyond marriage, Ruth is asking Boaz to become her kinsman-redeemer (see an explanation on page 68). With all of the favors being asked of Boaz, you might expect him to back down or seek immoral favors from Ruth. Instead he proclaims his joy at her offer, expresses his willingness for the role as kinsman-redeemer, and tells her when to leave so that her own reputation isn't tarnished. It's clear that God has great plans for these two!

6. Immediately after expressing his willingness to be their kinsman-redeemer, he immediately informs Ruth that there is a closer relative who has the legal right to such a position, should he decide to accept. When the new candidate first hears of the offer, he is willing to take on the responsibility of Elimelech's property. However, when he learns that he will also have to take care of Ruth and her mother-in-law, he simply cannot accept, lest he incur damage to his own property and future. Now Boaz can take on Ruth, Naomi, and all of the land that comes with them. This formal meeting, which seems to us an unnecessary precaution, is actually the Bible's way of showing us that this relationship is blessed by God. The events that follow will render this extra material necessary.

   We also have kinsman-redeemers in our lives. Most of us can think of at least one person who cared for us and helped us when we were in trouble and had nothing to give back. Perhaps your spouse has been there for you and loved you even when you considered yourself a complete wreck. Maybe an aunt, uncle, or grandparent has stepped in and acted as a parent to you in the absence of your own. We all have stories of people who have shown us great kindness when we truly needed it. Perhaps you have been a kinsman-redeemer yourself.

   Christ is, of course, our great Kinsman-Redeemer. He has redeemed us, not from a life of physical poverty, but from an eternity in hell. We can never do enough in this life to earn our own salvation. We deserve hell, and that is exactly what we have to look forward to outside of Christ. Jesus, however, came to earth, took on human flesh, and died for our sins. We see in the Galatians passage that the law would have crushed us if not for Christ. In Peter's epistle, we read that we were redeemed with Christ's blood, which is far more precious than gold or silver. Boaz was a great man who made a huge impact on Ruth's life. However, none of that would have been possible if not for the great Kinsman-Redeemer, Jesus Christ.

7. The grandson of Ruth and Boaz was none other than King David, who would forever be remember as the greatest king that Israel ever had. David's ancestor (and consequently, the ancestor of Boaz and Ruth) is our Lord and Savior, Jesus Christ. That's right! Ruth is the great- (not sure how many greats) grandmother of Jesus Christ, the Son of God. Did she know this during her life? No. In fact, much of her life was spent in poverty and suffering. As I quoted earlier from **Romans 5**, we as Christians can rejoice in those sufferings, however, knowing that they are all part of God's plan. Ruth had to be molded and shaped so that she would be an appropriate wife for Boaz. Their son, Obed, had to be born so that the line of Jesus Christ could continue.

    This says quite a bit about our own lives as well. You might see yourself as completely ordinary. You might not be able to pinpoint God's blessings in your life. You might even die without ever fully seeing or understanding God's plan for you. However, God does have a plan for you (**Jeremiah 29:11**), and His plan will exceed anything you could ever imagine or create for yourself. Glory be to God!

Nicodemus

1. Some of us might like to imagine that we'd have something very clever to say. No doubt Nicodemus thought that he was very clever when he first approached Christ. The thing about Jesus, however, is that He makes all of our wisdom look like foolishness. I once use to picture myself asking Him all sorts of questions. After studying this account, however, I think that now I would just keep quiet and listen. What could we possibly add to the conversation? It should be noted, however, that Nicodemus's buffoonery leads to one of the greatest and clearest explanations of Baptism in the entire Bible, as well as what some refer to as the "Gospel in a nutshell" (**John 3:16**).

2. As a Pharisee, Nicodemus would have been a scholar in the law. He would have had, at minimum, a working knowledge, and probably a vast knowledge of Jewish law and the Old Testament. By virtue of his calling, he was one of the brightest minds among the Jews. Despite all of this, however, he couldn't add one thing of worth to the conversation with Jesus. He misunderstood the grace of God in Baptism (**3:4**) and doubted God's abilities (**3:9**).

   Even with lifelong study and practice in the law of the Old Testament, Nicodemus couldn't wrap his mind around God's grace in Baptism. This shows that we are not able to understand anything in the Bible (and least of all the Sacraments or grace) without the enlightenment of the Holy Spirit. Centuries of church history have proven that oftentimes the most brilliant and scholarly minds are the ones that become the most confused when it comes to Biblical matters. That's why the Bible tells us more than once to have faith like a child (**Psalm 8:2, Matthew 18:1-6**)!

3. This text has historically been interpreted in a couple of different ways. Those who embrace a decisional theology say that to be born again, you have to make a decision for Christ. I find it ironic that anyone would credit himself with the ability to choose Baptism in light of Nicodemus's own misunderstanding. This text is beautifully framed by man's misunderstanding because Baptism is such a difficult concept for us to understand. The Greek word (ἄνωθεν), which can be interpreted as "born again" or "born from above," is the stumbling block. However, Jesus is speaking here of a spiritual birth. Just as Jesus initiates the conversation about Baptism with Nicodemus, so God also initiates the act of Baptism in our lives. Because of our sin, we cannot choose Baptism. God works faith in us through the water and His Word to receive this gift. And what a gift it is!

    When I state that we die and are raised again to life, I am simply repeating the wisdom of Paul in his letters to the Romans and to Titus. Baptism is no mere ritual. We are not making a decision to join in the family of God when we are baptized. Rather, when we are baptized, we are purged of the evil spirit (**Titus 3:4-7**) that has been inside of us since the fall in the Garden of Eden (**Genesis 3:22-24**). We are filled with God's own Spirit, which produces faith within us. This is all God's work. Since God is the one at work here, we gladly and openly baptize infants, wanting all of these benefits to be worked in them as well.

4. The work of the Holy Spirit is to call, gather, enlighten, and sanctify the Christian church here on earth. (Read Luther's Explanation of the Third Article of the Apostle's

Creed from the Small Catechism.) The Spirit brings us closer to Christ by constantly reminding us of our need for a Savior and showing us that Christ is the only way. Throughout the history of the church, however, the Holy Spirit's role in converting sinners, as well as man's role as a vessel, has been confused.

There are a couple of different ways to misunderstand this relationship. The first is to assume that the Holy Spirit and God's Word cannot work and convert unbelievers apart from our own efforts. Proponents of this thinking are convinced that without their own "witness," God's Word is dead and lifeless. The second false view is that God doesn't use Christians in the conversion of unbelievers at all. How can this be, when God has placed so many unbelievers into our lives, so that we can use our own life situations and relationships to share His Word with them? No, we must finally realize that the Holy Spirit works through man in the conversion of unbelievers.

This reasoning should be tempered with the knowledge that God doesn't *need* our help. He could raise stones to spread His message of salvation (**Luke 19:40**). Despite this, and the fact that we could only hinder His message in our human sinfulness, God wants us to spread His Word. He uses us as vessels of His truth. He places individuals in our lives who are in need of His Word. He sets the stage and lets us give an account for the faith that we have. What a great God to give us such a wonderful responsibility!

Even though our own human frailty cannot add to the Message, God's Word works by the power of the Holy Spirit. What comfort! Take this knowledge and spread the Word of God, knowing that your ability or inability to speak eloquently has no effect in the conversion of unbelievers. Instead, God works through us, giving us the Word and the power that we need to tell others the Good News (**Mark 13:11**).

5. If you have a difficult time remembering Scripture, there are a few things that you can do. Martin Luther would suggest learning his Small Catechism, which directly highlights the most essential aspects of the Bible in a very simple way. You would learn the Ten Commandments, the Apostle's Creed, the Lord's Prayer, as well as essential truths about Baptism, Confession/Absolution, and the Lord's Supper. Luther provides plenty of Biblical texts to support his views. He actually wrote the Small Catechism as a way for pastors of his day to teach their parishioners. We use it today to teach our youth (and adults) what the life of a Christian is all about (which is Christ, of course!).

   Most of us, however, still find the Catechism a little daunting. We want an even shorter and simpler way to confess what we believe! Jesus is one step ahead of us – He beautifully summarizes the entire Christian faith in **John 3:16 (and 3:17-21)**, one of the greatest explanations of God's grace in the entire Bible. In this concise passage, we learn that God sent Christ, His Son, into the world to save us from sin and death. We are saved by grace through faith because of what Christ has done! You can share this with others without knowing how to dissect Paul's letters or paraphrase the Christological symbolism of the Old Testament (that's a mouthful!). Everything you need is right here in this one verse! Therefore, since God has made it so easy, be bold and fearlessly share the hope of life everlasting that you have in Christ!

Solomon

1. The birth of Solomon marked the end of God's anger against his servant, David. We know David as God's star – His chosen. God allowed David, then a humble shepherd, to slay the giant Goliath, to take over Saul's position on the throne of Israel, and to rule as Israel's greatest king. However, David had greatly sinned with Bathsheba, Uriah's wife. He had committed adultery, murder, and other sins as well in order to take Uriah's wife as his own. Upon confessing his guilt and sin, he learned from the prophet Nathan that his child would die. Supposing his heir to be the prophesied Messiah (Jesus is often called the Son of David – **Matthew 1:1**, **Mark 10:48**, **Luke 20:41**), he despaired of this new reality. He wondered if God's favor had left him.

   David mourned greatly for his firstborn with Bathsheba until the child's inevitable death. Only when Solomon – his second child with Bathsheba – had been born was he absolutely sure that he had been forgiven. Although David mistakenly thought that Solomon would be the Messiah, he was correct in assuming that God's favor was with him once more. Solomon's other name, Jedidiah, means "loved by the Lord." It was clear that God intended great things for this child (**2 Samuel 7:12-16**). And He did.

2. Instead of simply acquiring the throne from his father, Solomon finds himself in a bind. His older half brother Adonijah, seeking an opportunity, had already seized the crown for himself. **1 Kings 1:6** adds insult to injury by insinuating that David wasn't an attentive parent. Because of his neglect, Adonijah and some of Solomon's other brothers turned out to be corrupt.

It should be noted that Solomon wasn't even the eldest brother, so technically the throne shouldn't have been given to him. However, God had ordained that Solomon would be the descendant of David who would carry on the Messianic promise (see **2 Samuel 7:12-16**). Solomon, by the working of the Holy Spirit – with some help from his mother (Bathsheba) and David's pastor (Nathan the prophet) – eventually overturned Adonijah's faulty claim for the throne and became king himself (**1 Kings 1:46-48**). Assuming the rule of Israel was his first step toward becoming king. The second would come when he finally dealt with his older brother, the usurper – Adonijah.

Solomon's first act as king proved his worthiness beyond a doubt. Nobody deserved death as much as Adonijah at that moment. He had tried to go against God's promise and take what was not his. Solomon would have been justified in the eyes of his people for taking Adonijah's life. He would have had everyone's best interest in mind. However, his bold statement of mercy (**1:52-53**) shows wisdom beyond his years and perhaps a divine right to the throne. He truly is God's chosen king!

3. This is one of the best known accounts from Solomon's life. What impresses us the most is the amazing generosity of God's offer. Solomon has so pleased God that He now offers him *anything* he could want! It's difficult for us to know what we'd ask for if presented with such an opportunity. We might wish for health, for life, for wealth and power, or just for love. Solomon, already displaying a wisdom that few of us could fathom, asks only for the wisdom and discernment to lead God's people. He certainly possessed the heart of a king.

Solomon's request also gives us a powerful model for our own individual prayers. We see in **Matthew 21** that everything asked for in prayer will be delivered, if we have faith. We fail to show faith when we ask God to give us more material possessions or happiness on this earth. His Word has revealed that life on this earth will be difficult (**1 Peter 1:6, James 1:2**). However, when we ask for the discernment to use the gifts which we've already been given, this is a pleasing request. As God says in His Word, those who ask for such things will be able to move mountains (**Matthew 21:21**).

4. Solomon is God's "golden boy." He is the blessed king of Israel, and is even given the privilege of building God's temple. God has given him wisdom beyond every other person on the planet. In addition to this wisdom, Solomon is granted wealth and power unsurpassed by anyone before or after his reign. Solomon seemed untouchable – an extraordinary human being if ever there was one.

His power, however, became his downfall. Seeking pleasure in all the wrong ways, Solomon acquired over a thousand lovers. He certainly committed adultery in the midst of his life-long orgy, but that was not his most deplorable sin. The Bible clearly states in **1 Kings 11:9** that Solomon's lovers turned him from God. He began to pray to their gods in addition to his own. He divided his heart among the various deities, forgetting that God is a jealous God who demands our entire heart (**Exodus 20:2-3**). Solomon was guilty of breaking the first commandment, which is the greatest and most grievously broken (**Matthew 27:37-38**).

We fall victim to the same sins in our own lives. We may not sleep around with multiple lovers, but that's hardly the point. There are many things in this life that pull our focus away from God. Money, pursuit of happiness, power, and even our families can distract us and take us away from loving God with our whole heart. When our focus on Christ is lost, the devil sneaks in for the kill. Remember that Satan is a prowling lion (**1 Peter 5:8**). He's cleverer than any one of us. He outsmarted Solomon with his lies, and we are no match for his deceit either. Indeed, our situation seems bleak.

One did come, however, who would change that situation forever. It doesn't matter that Satan is far more powerful than we are, because God sent His own Son, Jesus Christ, into this world to die on the cross and defeat sin and Satan (**Genesis 3:15**). God will protect us in the midst of our sufferings and temptations (**1 Corinthians 10:13**). By His strength, Satan is crushed (**Romans 16:20**). We receive God's strength, through Christ, when we gather together to hear God's Word and receive His Sacraments. By His gifts we are sustained, until we are delivered from this valley of sorrow that we call earth, into His heavenly arms.

5.   Solomon has greatly angered God. The kingdom which was promised to his father David is in danger of being stripped away. However, on account of David's virtue and faithfulness, Solomon doesn't lose the kingdom during his lifetime. However, he has to live with the guilt of knowing that his son will lose almost everything on account of *his* sinful mistakes! Also, for the sake of David, God gives Solomon's successor one tribe through which the Messianic line will be preserved. We can see that in spite of the inability of man to trust God's promises, God has infinite mercy and sends a Savior anyway.

Most of us have stories of someone else taking the fall for us. For many of us, this will conjure up images of childhood, where we let a sibling or friend get punished for something that we did wrong. We fled from the justice that we knew we ourselves deserved. As adults, we sometimes see this happen as well. However, we also feel a tremendous guilt over our unconfessed sin and long to let the truth be known. God will forgive us if we only come to Him, laying our sins at His feet. The life of a Christian is a life of repentance. God knows that we sin. He knows that we cannot overcome sin, death, and the devil on our own. He has sent His Son into this world, to be our Savior, and to mediate for us for all time (**Hebrews 2:18**).

6. Solomon was born into privilege. He was chosen by God for the throne of Israel. He was allowed to build God's house on earth. God granted him amazing wisdom, wealth, and power. All of these gifts, however, are dwarfed by the gift of the Promise. This Promise, first offered to Adam, working through Abraham, Ruth, David, and now Solomon, was the promise that one of their descendants would be the Messiah.

   This Messiah, both God and man, would be born of a virgin, live a humble life, die on a cross, and rise again, triumphing over Satan and hell. Jesus Christ is Solomon's greatest legacy!

7. None of us will ever experience the level of wealth, power, or wisdom that Solomon possessed. Most of us feel very ordinary by comparison. However, even Solomon showed his ordinary character by falling from God's grace and losing the kingdom of Israel. Learning from his example, we see that nobody is safe from the shortcomings of sin. We are all doomed to fail of our own accord. There appears to be very little comfort for us in this life. And then we read **Matthew 6:28-34**.

In this beautiful passage from Matthew, we read Solomon's name. He is compared to a lily of the field. We read that God gives great beauty to even the simplest of creation. If so much attention to detail is given to a flower, which can be plucked from the ground or destroyed at a whim, how much more must God care about humans, His most personal creation! We are endowed with the very breath of God (**Genesis 2:7**). We can be certain that in this life, as well as in the next, God has our greatest good in mind. He will always protect, sustain, and care for us until the very end. Don't worry about tomorrow. Tomorrow will worry about itself.

Zacchaeus

1. Everyone has at least one person in his or her life that possesses the characteristics of a hero. Perhaps some will see their mother or father as a hero. These are people who care for us, defend us, and mirror the love that God has for us. Others will see mighty warriors and protectors, such as firefighters and police officers, as heroes. No matter who we consider our heroes, we must understand that none of these people are allowed to do anything apart from Christ. As Paul says in Philippians, Christ is the source of his strength. That same Jesus Christ is the source of *your* strength as well. Imagine the possibilities!

2. Zacchaeus is a chief tax collector from the city of Jericho. This position and geography are clear signs to the reader (as well as Luke's own admission in **verse 19:2**) that Zacchaeus was a very wealthy man. We will cover the significance of this occupation in later questions. However, it's important to know what background Zacchaeus comes from before describing why his actions were so strange!

3. We just learned that Zacchaeus – a chief tax collector – is a man of wealth and power. Tax collectors were despised because their very presence meant that money would be changing hands. Even so, people respected the results of their labor. As such, Zacchaeus should have been able to elbow his way through the crowds to see Jesus. His height might have acted as an inhibitor, but his status would have been sufficient. Instead of "throwing his weight around," Zacchaeus humbled himself by rushing to a nearby tree and climbed right up. He recognizes the

importance of a meeting with Jesus and will do anything to see Him. His perspective is already changing.

We have all done things and acted in ways that we are not proud of. Our mouths slip on the worst of occasions (**James 3:5-6**) and we constantly fail to fulfill God's Word (**Matthew 5:48**). In other words, we know that we don't measure up. God's law teaches us that we are sinners in need of a Savior. We often realize this in the depths of our despair. Our comfort is found in passages like **Luke 5:31-32**, where Christ explains that He came to die for sinners *like us*! You don't go to the doctor when you're healthy. Likewise, you don't need to go to church to receive God's forgiveness and gifts of Word and Sacrament if you're not a sinner. But the reality is that we are all sinners in need of a Savior (**Romans 3:23-24**). Recognizing this need is the beginning of true wisdom – and salvation! This is exactly what Paul tells us in **2 Corinthians 12** (especially **verses 9 and 10**). Indeed, this is extraordinary news for all of us ordinary people!

4. It's one thing to say that you are sorry. It's quite another to prove that you are, in fact, truly repentant for what you have done. For example, you may truly be sorrowful over an event or action. You might be sorry that you did it, and you might be sorry that you got caught. Either way, what good is it if you fall right back into the same sin and keep sinning (**John 8:11**)? There is something to be said for earnestly struggling against recurring sins (i.e., addictions to pornography, drugs, etc.). True repentance bears fruit, which is the work of God.

Zacchaeus has shown, by God's grace, his earnest repentance by attempting to right many of the wrongs that he has committed throughout his life (**Luke 19:8**). He isn't doing this to secure his salvation. That has been won for him already, completely outside of his own efforts. On the contrary, he now recognizes his sins against God and the needs of his fellow man. He desires to give to his neighbor some of the generous love that has been shown to him by God through Jesus Christ. His offering of money and reparations is only one small step toward fully understanding the self-sacrificing love of Jesus Christ (**John 15:9-17**), which only God can provide and which we will never fully attain in this life on earth.

True repentance bears fruit. However, repentance is a daily reality in our lives, as the old sinful nature in us is "drowned" through the miracle of God's Word and holy Baptism (**Romans 6:3-4**). We mustn't think that we are ever done with sinning or repentance. These will be our reality until the last day, when our Lord delivers us from this valley of sorrows and brings us to Himself in heaven. For although sin and repentance are our temporal reality, there is no greater reality than Jesus Christ. Our victory is in Him.

5. While the term "son of Abraham" may mean nothing to you, it was a title of high distinction among Jews in Jesus' time. To call someone such as Zacchaeus, who was a despicable tax collector, a son of Abraham was a terrible insult to those who felt that this distinction rightly belonged only to them. Jews had long held the belief that the righteous among them were truly men after the tradition of Abraham. To be God fearing and law abiding, according to their traditions, meant a life of difficult labor and walking the path of God. Therefore, a common sinner like Zacchaeus would never be considered.

This entire order started to crumble with the incarnation of our Lord, Jesus Christ. We recall the Pharisees coming to receive John the Baptist's Baptism

(**Luke 3:7-9**). John knew that they were driven by false motives. These Jewish men of the law felt that they deserved salvation simply because they were of the right lineage. John boldly asserted that birthright isn't enough. He said that God could raise children of Abraham from the stones (**3:8**). Despite John's warning, this mindset prevailed among the religious Jews of the age.

Jesus further muddied the distinction when He announced this title upon Zacchaeus, a public sinner. In doing so, He forgave Zacchaeus all of his sins. Paul describes the new order in **Galatians 3:6-9**, pointing out that it was Abraham's faith, not his lineage, that made him a child of God. So we also are children of Abraham and God when we remain faithful to His promise in Jesus Christ. Zacchaeus' bold proclamation of faith makes him a true son of Abraham and a true hero of the faith!

Rahab

1. Perhaps the best analogy concerning the law and our salvation comes from Martin Luther. He states that the law is necessary, because it shows us that we are sick (in our sin) and in need of a cure.[8] That same law, however, cannot cure us. We need the Gospel of Jesus Christ, our Savior, to provide the cure (**John 3:16-21**). Many would dispute this fact, but there is more than ample evidence in Scripture that this is true. The passages that I've included from **Galatians 2** and **Hebrews 10** provide a clear explanation of the law and how it is not profitable for salvation, although necessary in our lives as children of God (**Ephesians 2:10**).

   If the law doesn't save us (and it doesn't), then it becomes necessary to understand what does. Only the Gospel, which cleanses us (**John 15:3**) and makes us children of God, can save us through the work of Jesus Christ, who is the Word made flesh (**John 1:1-18**). Read **John 15:13-15** and also Martin Luther's explanation of the third article of the Apostle's Creed (Small Catechism) for a better understanding of how God calls us to faith in Jesus Christ through the power of the Holy Spirit.

2. The whole discussion concerning the fear of God is a stumbling block for many. Why would we fear a God who loves us and only wants the best for us? However, it is good to possess a fear of God. All throughout the Bible, we read that a fear of God is necessary in true

---

[8] Luther, Martin. *Luther's Works, Volume 43: Devotional Writings II*, G.K. Wiencke, Ed. (pp. 13-14). Philadelphia: Fortress, 1968.

believers. The important distinction, however, is how that fear is placed.

Some fear God as the third servant in the Parable of the Talents (**Matthew 25:24-30**), supposing that God will zap us for every little mistake that we make. As you can see in this Parable, spoken by the mouth of Christ Himself, God is not pleased with this kind of fear. No, God desires for us to fear Him as children fear their father.

Think back to your childhood. Were you ever afraid of your father? Whenever we did something that we were not supposed to do, we feared the consequences of that decision. However, we also knew that our fathers loved us and didn't really want to hurt us. Any punishment that we received was for our own learning and growth. If our fathers knew how to treat us so that we would grow up to be successful and mature adults, how much more does God know what we need as His children (**Luke 11:11-13**)!

3. What is right is not always popular. What is popular is not always right. These simple words were probably first introduced to you as a child, when such teachings are most beneficial. Our school years provided many opportunities to choose between doing what was popular and what was right. In my high school, for example, it was popular to sleep around and drink alcohol heavily on the weekends. On more than one occasion, I saw my classmates drink themselves within an inch of alcohol poisoning. Why? Because they thought it would help them to fit in – to form an identity.

    Promiscuity and underage drinking were the rights of passage in my small town. I stayed away from both and was unpopular because of my decisions. I'm sure we all have personal examples of when we made a decision to go along with the crowd, even when it was the wrong thing to do. Thankfully, Rahab made the right decision. The consequences of her decision were far more important than just who she was able to hang around with at school or work. This was a life and death situation.

In Rahab's time, the worth of a prostitute in the eyes of society probably wasn't much more than it is today. The king could have killed her without even a twinge of guilt. He does, however, offer her a special privilege in acting as a snitch for the great city of Jericho. Rahab has the opportunity to tattle on these foreign spies and become a town hero! Think of all the business such fleeting fame could bring her! Despite this, she chooses the spies (and, more notably, their God) in a decision that could very well have cost her life. However, no trust placed in God is ever in vain. She saw that her brave king in his mighty walls was terrified of this God, and she realized that He was worth dying for. The result? Her change of heart (created in her by God) brought her a lifetime of fame and notoriety, becoming one of only three women mentioned in the genealogy of Jesus Christ.

4. Rahab, displaying both an innocent understanding of God's might and also a strong faith toward a God that she didn't fully understand, was saved from the destruction of Jericho (**Joshua 6:25**), while the other inhabitants were completely destroyed (**Joshua 6:21**).

We read in **Matthew 18**, in the midst of the Apostles' overblown egos, that children are blessed in heaven. Not only children, but those who espouse a faith like a child. This faith is completely trusting in God for every good thing. This faith also fears God appropriately and does not test Him to anger (**Matthew 4:7**).

But then Paul comes in, saying in **1 Corinthians** that we must put off our childish ways and that we must

mature in our faith (**3:1-2**). What seems to be a contra-
diction is also a completion of Rahab's characteristics.
You see, she did display a childlike faith, but she also
showed great cunning and intelligence when she reasoned
with Joshua's spies for safe passage (**Joshua 2:12-13**).
We are not called to be simpletons in this life. Indeed,
any of you with enough knowledge of children will know
that they are quite advanced in their capacity to learn.
Instead, we are called to be clever and wise, always
holding fast to the faith that we've been given (**Matthew
10:16**). It's not an easy calling, to be sure, but it's the
greatest honor in this life.

5. Rahab's story ends very well. She and her family are the
sole survivors of the Jericho massacre. Joshua even tells
us that she lived out her days among believers. She is
bequeathed with honors that most of us will never realize
in this life. In short, she has a happy ending.

Not all believers will experience that kind of joy
in this present life. In fact, believers have a much harder
life than unbelievers. God gives all manner of good
things to everyone, regardless of belief (**Matthew 5:45b**),
but believers become prime targets for Satan's deceptions.
Satan is a prowling lion (**1 Peter 5:8**), waiting to snare us
in one of his traps. He wants nothing more than to
separate us from our heavenly Father. As such, Baptized
Christians may often have a difficult time in this life.

We are hated and persecuted because Christ was
first hated and persecuted (**John 15**). As we read in the
Bible, Christ was hated without a cause (**Psalm 35:19**).
So we also must expect hardship in this life. As we just
covered in question 4, however, God is allowing this to
happen to us so that we might grow and mature in our
faith. We rejoice in these trials, knowing that our sufferings cannot last (**John 16**). No matter what happens to us

in this life, we look forward, with certainty, to an eternity in heaven with our Savior. This is a reward reserved for believers alone. Glory be to God!

Hannah

1. While we cannot relate to Hannah's marital situation (one
    of two wives in a polygamous marriage), some of us *can*
    relate to her barrenness, and most of us can remember
    times in our lives when we felt forgotten. These may
    have been times of extreme hardship, when we felt as if
    our support group was nowhere to be found. They may
    also have been times when we were lonely, with no one
    around to comfort us. In times like these, it's pretty easy
    to feel as if God is elsewhere as well. After all, it's
    natural to think that if God was near us, we wouldn't be
    so miserable!

    Throughout the Bible, we see passages of comfort
    (such as **Deuteronomy 31** and **Jeremiah 29**) that promise
    God's presence in our lives. God is always around to care
    for us and He always knows what we need. Unfortu-
    nately, we don't possess God's wisdom or foresight, and
    we don't understand why certain things happen in our
    lives. He may be testing us now to shape us for the future
    (**Psalm 66:10**). One thing we can be certain of, however,
    is our salvation through Jesus Christ. The hope that we
    have for our future in heaven is greater than any sorrows
    in this life (**Revelation 2:10**).

2. Hannah would have been justified if she had responded in
    anger to Eli. This belligerent priest, ignorant of Hannah's
    barren womb, marital problems, and extreme depression,
    has accused her of being a drunkard. Instead of putting
    Eli in his place, which probably wouldn't have done any
    good anyway, she defends herself and begs Eli to change
    his opinion of her. This reminds us of what Peter writes
    in **1 Peter 2:12** concerning the lives of Christians. Eli
    and his family were not without fault themselves

(**1 Samuel 2:29**). Hannah easily could have accused Eli of poor behavior, but she doesn't. She holds her tongue.

We read in **Isaiah 53** (which gives an amazing description of Christ) that Jesus also didn't raise His voice against His accusers, but took the punishment that God had laid aside for Him. He defended Himself when necessary (**Luke 22:66-71**), but saw His sufferings as God's will (**Matthew 26:39**).

The most important work that Christ did involved His death on the cross, and His resurrection. We cannot follow in those footsteps. We can, however, learn from the example that Jesus led in His earthly life. Christ was gentle yet firm, kind yet driven. He taught what needed to be taught and said what needed to be said. Most importantly, He did what needed to be done. We can, with boldness, live lives worthy of Christians, sharing God's Word with others and following in the footsteps of Hannah, and especially of Jesus Christ.

3. It's all too easy for us to compare ourselves with others. We all have friends and family members whose accomplishments outshine our own. There will always be someone more talented, more beautiful, more intelligent, or more powerful. This is the way of the world. God made each of us unique and everyone possesses his or her own gifts and abilities (**Matthew 25:14-30**). However, the passage from **Matthew 10** should destroy any notions we may have about our lives simply being a supportive role for others.

You certainly support and strengthen others in your life, and are expected to do so (**1 Thessalonians 5:11**), but God is concerned with your individual life as well. He knows every hair on your head. God cares for each individual bird of the sky, and yet He will care for you much more than a simple sparrow. You are the star of God's show. So are your children, spouse, parents, co-workers, and neighbors. Everyone is equally loved and cared for in God's sight. Whether you're the servant who has been given five talents or one millionth of a talent, God has great plans for you (remember **Jeremiah 29:11**)!

4. Praying is somewhat of a mystery to many people. They often wonder what the best and most effective methods of prayer are. There is no denying the immense power of prayer (**Matthew 21**). Of course, our best example of prayer comes directly from Jesus' own mouth, in the Lord's Prayer (**Matthew 6:9-13**). These words are perfect, and should be said every day. Hannah's example, however, provides us with even more information regarding God-pleasing prayer.

　　　As in the Lord's Prayer, Hannah addresses God by His name. God wants us to come to Him as His children. Therefore, we should begin our prayers with such addresses as "Our Father." We don't do this for God's benefit, but for ours, so that we always remember the nature of our relationship with Him. Also, Hannah weeps and opens her heart emotionally before God. Our tears will not motivate God any more than the crocodile tears of a small child desiring candy will motivate a stalwart parent trying to get him to eat his broccoli. However, God loves it when we pray in all sincerity to Him. Even when we don't know what to pray, or are in such pain that all we can muster are groans and utterances, God promises to hear us. These whispers and murmurs, from deep within our hearts, are the work of the Holy Spirit **(Romans 8:26-27)**, who perfects our weak and ignorant desires.

　　　Perhaps most striking of all about Hannah's prayers is the joy that she proclaims in the Lord, despite the fact that she will have to give up her beloved and long-awaited child (**1 Samuel 2:1**). Unlike Mary, who was able to keep the baby Jesus, or David, who proclaimed with such joy after a great military victory, Hannah is rejoicing in the face of loss. This is another great example for us. We cannot simply praise God when things go well and curse Him when things go poorly for us (**Job 1:21**). God is good no matter what situations our sin drives us into. God is good no matter what trials we face in this life. God is *always* worthy of praise. Hannah understood this. We would do well to follow her example.

5. I love this comparison. Abraham is praised from the beginning of the Old Testament until the end of the New Testament for his great faith. And a great faith it was. Abraham was a man who was willing to kill his long-awaited and only son to honor God. Passages such as **Hebrews 11:19** show us that Abraham believed that God would bring his son back to him or give him another, but passages like **James 2:21-23** teach us that Abraham's willingness to sacrifice was a great work nonetheless. Hannah, however, gets very little mention for her sacrifice.

Hannah is never praised in the New Testament for her sacrifice. Although he lived, she did indeed sacrifice Samuel. After suffering a barren womb for so many years, Hannah now had to give up *her* long-awaited son to honor God. This sounds familiar. Hannah's story is nearly equal to that of Abraham. God opened her womb, just as He had with Sarah, but the baby was to be considered His, and not the female womb that He used. Just as with Abraham, God wanted to see if He was more important to her than her new child. Hannah, the faithful servant, gave up Samuel to God's service (**1 Samuel 1:22**).

6. God blessed Hannah exceedingly for her sacrifice and obedience. Instead of living alone and dejected, Hannah was blessed with three sons and two daughters. Although she was once barren, God has given her and Elkanah six beautiful children. Samuel may not have the opportunity to grow up living with his parents, but he will grow up to perform marvelous deeds in the sight of God. Very few in the Bible are more blessed than Hannah.

7. Most people only remember that Job lost all of his possessions, including his children, and suffered greatly. Few remember that not only did God return what had been taken from Job, but He gave him back *twice* what was taken! Job was doubly blessed for his obedience and faith.

    We can be certain in this life that there will be suffering. We suffer because of sin, and the only cure for sin is to die in faith to Jesus Christ. Once we have been taken from this sinful world, we will live in perfect bliss – in heaven – for all eternity. Jesus, dying on the cross and rising again for the salvation of the entire world, has made this possible for us. We can do nothing to perfect ourselves in the eyes of God. Only Christ could, and did, accomplish this as God's perfect Son.

    While we are certain that there will be suffering in this world, we can also be certain of our heavenly reward in Christ. Hannah lived in sorrow, as did Job. Neither of them, however, lost sight of God and His love for them. The result is that God rewarded them richly (**1 Corinthians 1:3-5**), blessing them with a happy end in this life. I've stated before that we won't always see a happy ending in this world. Satan is a powerful adversary and his entire being is devoted to making us miserable and trying to turn us away from God. However, when we die, we will be separated from Satan, hurt, sorrow, and death for all of eternity. We will truly be home! In the words of Hannah, mother of Samuel the prophet: **"There is no one holy like the Lord; there is no one besides you; there is no Rock like our God"** (1 Samuel 2:2). Amen, Hannah. Amen!

The Widow of Zarephath

1. All of us can think back to at least one moment in our lives when many obligations convened at once to demand our time. My example of graduation, postgraduate work, track meets, and finals isn't unique. Many student athletes go through this very situation every year. We are never going to be able to prevent these "perfect storms" from happening, but we *can* put our hope in God's Word, which promises that God will always provide a way out.

    Paul's words in **1 Corinthians 10** have always given me great comfort in the midst of my afflictions. If God always provides a way out, then it's never as bad as we make it out to be. We often feel like we'll just cease to exist if one more person or event encroaches upon our time. However, God has uniquely planned our lives so that we might brush up against the brink of despair, but needn't ever cross over because of our faith in Jesus Christ. Christ has felt our pain (**Hebrews 2:18**), and He will always be there as our Mediator, Advocate, and Comforter to help see us through.

2. Elijah will always be remembered for his attack on the religion and priests of Baal (**1 Kings 18:20-40**). He so outraged the evil Queen Jezebel that she put a price on his head (**1 Kings 19:2-3**). It seems absurd to us that God would send his star prophet into the very heart of Baal country, to be served and waited upon by a pagan widow with barely a penny to her name. He had His reasons, however, which we will learn in the next few questions.

3. In **Matthew 22**, Christ informs a lawyer, who was sent by the Pharisees, that loving God above all and loving our neighbor as ourselves is the greatest goal in this life. We

accomplish this when we live our lives for others. It's important to note that this work we do for others isn't aiding in our salvation. Our salvation was won by Christ, apart from the law (**Ephesians 2:8-9**). In light of this salvation, however, God desires for us to live our lives for others. The widow of Zarephath provides an excellent example of this love.

This widow was at her wit's end. She didn't have any provisions for herself or her son. Baal, her god and the god of her people, had let her down. She was going to starve to death, miserable and unable to save her son. In the midst of her suffering, she receives a houseguest in the person of Elijah. She warns Elijah that there is not much to give, but she fulfills his request for food and drink anyway. She truly loves Elijah as she loves herself. She could die fulfilling his request, but she fulfills it anyway, displaying the love of Christ. Not bad for a pagan – although she won't remain a pagan for long.

We follow the widow's example when we give of ourselves to our friends and family in this life, as well as anyone who comes to us in need. That's right! Everyone we meet is our neighbor! You might have thought at first that you simply needed to watch out for the Jones' across the street or the Smiths next door. Actually, God has called for you to care for everyone that you meet, in both body and soul. When you provide safe lodging or food for someone in need of these items, you are nourishing his body for the present. When you share the Word of God with that same person, you are nourishing his soul for all eternity (**Matthew 4:4**). This is what it means to love your neighbor as yourself. Don't worry about your perceived inability to fulfill God's commission. The Holy Spirit will always be present in God's Word to intercede for you (**Acts 1:8**). Despite our own unworthiness, God's

Word will always reach its mark, just as it did with the widow from Zarephath.

4. Miracles have always fascinated people. Even those who do not believe in Jesus as their Lord still wonder how He performed all of those miracles. *How* did He turn water into wine (**John 2:1-11**)? *How* did He raise Lazarus from the dead (**John 11:38-44**)? *How* did He feed the 5,000 or walk on water (**Mark 6:30-56**)? Herein lies the problem. Those who reject Christ but marvel at His miracles are focusing on the "how." Instead of studying and attempting to explain the "how of each miracle, either through hard science or mere conjecture, we must focus on the "why." *Why* did Jesus turn water into wine, raise Lazarus from the dead, feed the 5,000, and walk on water?

Through such passages as **John 10** and **Hebrews 2**, we see that Jesus performed these miracles in order to show that He is God's incarnate Son, and that what He said is the truth. Christ's Word is the main focus here. The miracles are simply a testament to the validity of His message. And yes, such miracles happen even today.

Babies are born, weather appears and dissipates, and the universe displays phenomena that we can only attempt to explain. All of these things happen in order to show that God is a present and living reality in our lives. Going beyond natural wonders, we see the miracle of God's truth recorded perfectly in the Bible. Every page therein explains and proves the divinity of Jesus Christ, who took on human flesh and died so that we might live. This is the greatest miracle of all!

5. Certainly we would say that this widow finally *knows* that she has faith in **verse 24**, when she openly proclaims Elijah as a true prophet and his God as the One True God. I would argue, however, that she had faith even before she

knew it! In **verse 18**, when her son has stopped breathing and she is beginning to panic for his survival, she blurts out the most natural thing to her mind. She asks Elijah if God is punishing her because of her sin. Aha! As a pagan worshipper of Baal, she wouldn't have worried if Elijah's God had any problem with her. She wouldn't even have known that she was living outside of His grace. Indeed, things had changed.

We might assume that the widow had faith even when she was providing for Elijah and seeing the miracles of God shower upon her in the form of flour and oil. However, it took the death of her son for this woman to finally understand that she was a sinner and that Elijah's message was her only salvation. She immediately appealed to Elijah to save her son – which he does, by the grace of God. Elijah's resurrecting the boy, however, isn't the greatest miracle in this narrative.

As I mention on page 129, the true miracle is that this widow and her son are now believers who will live their lives for the God of Israel. It won't be an easy life, and it may become even more difficult because of chastisement from their pagan neighbors. However, the consequences of this new faith are eternal. Much greater than a return to earthly life from death, the widow and her son have received the resurrection that all believers experience – from eternal death into eternal life – through Jesus Christ.

6. It has been said that we need to put the Word of God into the hands of dynamic people. This is a true statement. However, assuming that only dynamic personalities can produce fruit from God's Word is against the teaching of the Bible. Instead, we need to focus on putting the dynamic Word of God into the hands of all people. Your Uncle Fred, Aunt Lois, and Cousin Ben are just as

capable of sharing the Word of God as the greatest evangelist.

The proof is found in such passages as **Hebrews 4** and **2 Timothy 3**. In these passages, we hear that God's Word is a living, breathing testament to His message of truth. Our ability or inability to speak eloquently and communicate adds nothing to this message. In short, God's Word does all of the work. However, God uses ordinary jars of clay (**2 Corinthians 4:6-7**), like us, as His vessels to convey His extraordinary message. As you've read throughout this book, God uses some pretty unlikely people to share His Word. Few of them would be considered dynamic. All of them were entrusted with the most precious message ever spoken.

Don't limit the work that you can accomplish by assuming that you're not equipped to share God's Word. Likewise, don't tell others that they aren't qualified to do so either. None of us are truly qualified to read, speak, or share God's Word. By the power of the Holy Spirit, however, this Word is our truth and our life. We thank God for using us as His vessels, just as He did with that ordinary widow in Zarephath.

Joseph

1. Most of us, at one point in our lives, have dreamed of winning the lottery. It's a temptation for us to ponder an existence with all the money we could ever want. It's amazing to me that more people buy tickets when the jackpot is larger. People have their reasons, however, and lottery tickets bring in considerable income for the states that participate.

    After winning the lottery, believe it or not, many people don't get what they expected. Winners often find themselves with more friends and family than they ever thought possible. Suddenly, they can't figure out who their real friends are, and which ones are attracted by the newfound wealth. Few people are prepared to handle this kind of sudden prosperity and all the situations and problems it may create, and it tears their personal lives apart. This brings to mind the phrase "be careful what you wish for." Note the wisdom of Jesus in **Matthew 19:23-24**. Wealth of possessions isn't everything.

    Joseph didn't ask to be wealthy. He didn't even ask to be the father figure for the Messiah. Regardless of what he thought he wanted or how he imagined his life unfolding, God had His own plans. Just as if he had won the lottery, Joseph's life would never be the same again. Most of the changes that Jesus brought into his life were drastic and challenging. Despite this reality, however, he fulfilled his duty to Mary and to God, fathering Jesus and raising Him to the best of his abilities.

2. It's rare in any culture for a man to stay with a fiancé who's been unfaithful and become pregnant, raising the child as his own. In the culture of Mary and Joseph, how-ever, it was unheard of. According to Levitical law, the

Godly thing to do would have been to bring Mary's evil actions into the open and to have her killed. Joseph, however, showing amazing faith and character, decided to leave her quietly.

Even in today's culture, with tolerance and freedom as war cries for any and every debauchery, it would be quite rare for a man to stand by his unfaithful betrothed and raise her illegitimate child. Also, the woman wouldn't be killed for her infidelity. She might even be looked upon as a heroine for bravely raising the child on her own.

Regardless of our culture's perceptions, Joseph's actions transcend all human reason. It's also important to note that Mary is not unfaithful to Joseph. She is, in fact, the only woman in all of history who ever conceives in this way. Jesus isn't Joseph's Son. He's the Son of God. Joseph, upon receiving God's reassurance (**Matthew 1:20-21**), considered it a higher honor to raise God's Son that any of his own. He rose to the challenge and cared for Jesus when He needed it the most.

3. I love Nativity scenes. I find great peace in the birth of my Savior and think that such remembrances are essential, especially during the Christmas season. Despite this, they hardly provide an adequate portrayal of Joseph and his family at the beginning of Christ's life. It seemed, at the very beginning, that nothing could go right.

The first of many terrifying ordeals manifested itself in the escape to Egypt. An angel appeared to Joseph, warning him that Herod was seeking to kill Jesus (**Matthew 2:13**). Next, they are returning home after the death of Herod when Joseph receives another dream warning him to stay away from Bethlehem (**Matthew 2:19-23**). It seems that Herod's son was no friend of the Christ Child, either. They then proceed to Nazareth, where Jesus grows into a Man. Jesus' troubles wouldn't end there, however. For the rest of His life, people would scorn and hate Him (**John 15:18**), finally hanging Him on a cross in utter humiliation. His death is our life. We rejoice in Jesus' death, knowing that He was raised from the grave after three days, defeating sin and Satan in the process. This reality provides far greater comfort than any plastic Nativity scene could ever hope to.

Just as a Nativity scene could never fully portray the birth of our Savior, so also can we see the major discrepancy between our own lives and what we see in a snow globe. People in a snow globe seem to live the perfect life. Children sled with their bright scarves and canine companions. Carolers sing in front of cozy dwellings with plumes of smoke rising from the friendly chimneys. Yes, everything looks great in a snow globe, but it doesn't match the pain and suffering that we feel in our lives. The real Christmas story is so much better because it does match our own experience, our own reality. We can truly rejoice in our sufferings (**Romans 5:3-5**), knowing that Christ suffered just as we do, and He knows exactly what we're going through (**Hebrews 2:18**). The plastic Jesus mold has been broken. Our Savior is a flesh and blood God/Man who will never leave us nor forsake us (**Deuteronomy 31:6**)!

4. Why should we listen to the Son of a carpenter? Isn't this the same Jesus who grew up just down the street from us? What makes Him so special? You can literally hear the accusations, most of them entirely unfair. None of the accusers seem to understand that factors such as location and birthplace don't mean anything. The accusations about Joseph, however, have more weight. If Jesus is truly the Son of God, it makes little sense that He would consider Joseph to be His father. Those who have

watched Jesus grow up would surely have a difficult time believing that He is now divine – although He's been divine from conception – and that He can now do miracles. Indeed, Jesus' upbringing was quite ordinary, and His normal parents acted as terrific camouflage for His divinity.

Likewise, our unique life situations create a similar challenge in our own attempts to spread the Word of God. People will tell us that we are too young to understand what we're saying – I've heard this one a few times. They'll say that we can't understand their life situation, because we grew up in the country/city/north/south. We're too poor or wealthy to possibly wrap our minds around their particular issues and struggles. Nothing could be further from the truth.

The truth is that God's Word transcends all of these worldly concerns. Don't let anyone tell you that you aren't qualified to share the Word of God with others. If it depended on our own abilities and qualifications, this might be true. However, God uses *all* believers to further His kingdom, and He desires disciples from all nations (**Matthew 28:19**). If this weren't so, do you think that Ruth, Rahab, Esther, Nicodemus, Zacchaeus, Jonah, Lydia, Elisha, Solomon, Zacchaeus, the widow at Zarephath, or even Joseph would have made any kind of difference? God's Word is sharper than any two-edged sword (**Hebrews 4:12**). Armed with His Word, we cannot fail. It's not up to us to fail. Therefore, be bold, sharing God's message of salvation with everyone you meet. You are uniquely gifted, by God, to share His message.

5. Joseph, an unlikely hero of the faith, showed his love for his family by sacrificing his own plans at every turn. When the angel told him that he would be the caretaker of

the Christ, he humbly accepted the responsibility (**Matthew 1:24**). When he was told to uproot his entire life and flee from Herod's impending wrath, he did (**Matthew 2:13-14**). When he was instructed to abandon his home and live out his days in Nazareth, he acquiesced to God's wishes (**Matthew 2:22-23**). Joseph obeyed God because he knew that the birth and life of Christ was far greater than his own goals and ambitions. He sacrificed himself for his wife and stepson, with no regard for his own desires. In other words, he loved them unconditionally.

You may or may not be able to name people from your own life who have sacrificed their own wants and desires for you. Most of us, however, have parents, spouses, or even children who have shown this kind of love for us. All people learn how to love by following God's example. God loves us far more than we could ever love Him or one another. By reading **John 3:16** and **15:13**, we see that God shows His love for us by sending His only Son, to be born of Mary (**Luke 2:6-7**), to suffer and die (**Mark 15:17-20, 37**), and to rise again (**Matthew 28:5-7**), destroying death in the process (**Romans 6:3-5**). God could have shown His love in any way He desired. He chose self-sacrifice. We follow this example in our own lives when we esteem the happiness and well being of others above our own.

APPENDIX A:
WHAT DOES ALL THIS HAVE TO DO WITH ME?

What good would this book be if it produced no change in your life? Surely I didn't write this with the intention that you would become a scholar or even a Biblical expert. However, this book is written for change. When God called me on that fateful car ride home during my junior year of college, everything changed for me. I was no longer someone who simply went to church, punched a time clock and left. I was now the kind of dedicated Christian that the Bible talks about. I read the Scriptures more and more to gain a greater understanding of God's purpose for me. I realize now that my life is to be lived for the Lord, and I've never been happier. One day lived for the Lord is worth a lifetime spent in pursuit of empty happiness (**Psalm 84:10**).

Every year, millions of us buy self-help books, hoping to improve some aspect of our lives. Ultimately, most of our goals are very short term. Perhaps we want to look great and be fit. Maybe we want more money and possessions, which we believe will make our lives more comfortable. We might even learn types of meditation which can relax us and allow us to feel rested. While these things might have their place, I can say with absolute certainty that none of them will amount to anything in the end. Listen to this wisdom from the mouth of our Lord and Savior, Jesus Christ. **"Do not store up for yourselves treasures on earth, where moth and rust destroy, and where thieves break in and steal. But store up for yourselves treasures in heaven, where moth and rust do not destroy, and where thieves do not break in and steal. For where your treasure is, there your heart will be also"** (Matthew 6:19-21). None of the things we seek after in this life will last. Only the love of Jesus Christ will prevail.

Why should we worry about eternal life right now? Wouldn't it be better to get fit, make some money, improve ourselves, and then seek Christ later, perhaps when we are a little more worthy of His love and attention? Whether or not this sounds silly to you, many find themselves immersed in this mindset. This mentality is exactly the thing that keeps most people from seeking God, even when they realize He's real. They don't believe that they are worthy of such immense love. The truth is that we *aren't* worthy, but nobody else ever has been, either. The good news for us is that we are instead deemed acceptable to God by our Savior, who has made us worthy through His death and resurrection. That's right! Jesus died, rose again from the dead, and ascended into heaven, where He reigns eternally with God the Father. With these actions, He took away the burden of our sin (**1 Corinthians 15**). This means that we *are* able to enjoy eternal life in spite of our shortcomings. We cannot make ourselves worthy. This is why self-help books and false religions are so hazardous. They encourage us to look inward and find strength inside of ourselves. The problem with this is that we're not strong in ourselves, and we can never understand the ways of God outside of God. The more we look inward, the further we wander away from real peace and tranquility. It's not that the life of a Christian is any easier than that of a non-Christian, but we possess something that non-Christians don't have. We have the assurance of life after death, and eternal joy and bliss with Jesus Christ in heaven.

How do you know when God is calling you? This can be a point of contention for some, but it doesn't have to be. God called me over and over throughout my childhood, teens, and early twenties, always working through pastors and other adults to guide me in the right direction. He also worked through my wife, Andrea, and the faith she had in my eventual coming around to know God. Almost every one of her friends told her to dump me, and she probably would have if it weren't for something deeper telling her to stick it out. The Lord knew that I needed to have her in my life, and He also knew that I would answer His call during spring break of my junior year of college. He knows when *you* will come home to Him as well. Maybe you've gone to church in the past and found it to be uncomfortable. Maybe you've seen Christians acting contrary to the Bible's teachings and found the whole system to be hypocritical. No matter what your reasons, God has *allowed* you to reject His call to service. This is your freedom as a human being affected by sin. With this freedom you have the power to come and hear the Message and also the power to reject it. God doesn't force anyone to become a Christian. When He comes to us, we don't need to do anything ourselves; we are to simply receive His gifts. If you feel a need to hear the message of salvation in the Bible or to be in church, don't ignore these signs. Embrace them and see them as a calling from God, not random feelings.

You don't have to devote your entire life to the church as a full time church worker, like I've decided to do. It's important to know that no matter what job we're working in this world, whether it be accounting, cleaning, or farming, God can and will use it for His purposes. Any and every vocation that we do for the glory of God is equally pleasing in His eyes.

I can't stress enough the importance of belonging to a church. Coming to church once a week may seem like a minimal commitment to you, but it can make all the difference in the world. That weekly routine of joining other believers in worship and receiving the Word and Sacraments (Baptism, Communion, Absolution/Forgiveness of sins) will create profound changes within you. You may not even be trying to change, but the Word that is preached by the pastor and the Communion of Christ's body and blood that you eat and drink actually have the presence of Christ in them. He's becoming part of you when you hear the Word and receive the Sacraments, and we, in turn, become part of Him. Thus we all become part of the same body, also known as the church: **"Now you are the body of Christ, and each one of you is a part of it"** (1 Corinthians 12:27). You can see that going to church is much more than putting your bottom in the pew, as I once thought. It's a place of reception. This reception is not for gifts of this world, but for heavenly and eternal gifts that we cannot receive anywhere else.

You are always welcome at church. Come as you are, and don't let a fear of the unknown deter you. In fact, you don't have to know a single verse from the Bible to attend church. Once there, you'll find an entire community of people who have dealt with the same situations you're going through and can lend a helping hand. These are folks who have been through the tough times of life and have found the church to be a place of abundant hope and peace, and a true comfort in times of pain and grief. The pastor is another source of guidance and encouragement in the church. As previously mentioned, the title "Pastor" means Shepherd. Each pastor has been called by Jesus Christ to watch over His church, which can also be called His "flock." Imagine yourself as a sheep in need of the care of a faithful shepherd. Your pastor has been called by the church he serves and by God to care for you and make sure that you're pointed in the right direction. If you feel overwhelmed in your attempts to read and understand the Bible, your pastor can help you get started and stay firm in your faith. Chances are, your pastor's story is similar to my own, and he was once lost himself. Everyone's story is slightly different, but *all* Christians (including your pastor) have been brought from death to life through the miracle of Baptism and God's holy Word: **"Don't you know that all of us who were baptized into Christ Jesus were baptized into his death? We were**

therefore buried with him through baptism into death in
order that, just as Christ was raised from the dead
through the glory of the Father, we too may live a new
life" (Romans 6:3-4). Most pastors can relate to your situation and can give you, by the grace of God, the help or advice
you need.

Look to your Christian friends for guidance as well.
If they are not able to help you themselves, they can certainly
lead you to a faithful pastor. Christians are called not only to
help one another, but to share this good news of Jesus Christ
with those who may not yet know the message: "In your
hearts set apart Christ as Lord. Always be prepared to
give an answer to everyone who asks you to give the
reason for the hope that you have. But do this with
gentleness and respect" (1 Peter 3:15). Indeed, your
Christian friends can tell you much about the comfort and
hope that they have in Christ Jesus.

Even if you already belong to a church and feel close
to God prior to reading this book, regular immersion in the
Bible (perhaps a chapter or two each day) will strengthen
your relationship with God and help you to know Him even
better. While the entire Bible is great for wisdom and
learning: "All Scripture is God-breathed and is useful for
teaching, rebuking, correcting and training in righteousness, so that the man of God may be thoroughly equipped
for every good work" (2 Timothy 3:16-17), I would first
direct you to the Gospels: Matthew, Mark, Luke, and John.
These four books speak directly about the life of Jesus Christ
and His ministry, beginning with His incarnation and birth
through Mary and the Holy Spirit, and recording all the way
to the crucifixion and resurrection, which saved us from our
sins. While these four are the beginning of the New
Testament and an excellent summary of Jesus' life, there are
other important books which are written by the various
apostles, who were Jesus' closest followers. I'd especially

like to recommend the books of Acts, Romans, and Galatians. Acts is a wonderful book about the beginning of the church after the death of Christ. Romans and Galatians provide a great summary concerning the beliefs of the church.

What does all of this have to do with being ordinary? I've found that one of the greatest road blocks people encounter on the path to a healthy and fulfilling spiritual life with Jesus Christ is that they think things have to be a certain way before they can commit. These folks witness "super Christians" who give their lives to help people know more about Jesus Christ, and they are intimidated. They also have a tough time relating to people in the Bible and even to people who go to church. I certainly hope by now you know that we're all equally "ordinary" in God's eyes. God plays no favorites. He sees only two kinds of people: those who believe in Jesus Christ as their Savior and those who don't. Those who believe in Christ will inherit the kingdom of heaven, while those who don't believe will face the fires of hell. No amount of earthly glory will tilt the scales in either direction, not for us and not for the men and women in the Bible.

For those in the church and even for those who have little or no experience with the Bible, the Gospel of Christ Jesus can be summed up in one verse recorded by the apostle John. **"For God so loved the world that he gave his one and only Son, that whoever believes in him shall not perish but have eternal life"** (John 3:16). The central message of the Bible is this: Jesus Christ came down from heaven, humbled Himself to be made man, and died at our hands so that all of our sins would be forgiven (we couldn't save ourselves). There are countless books and scholarly works written about this Message. Men live and die for this Message. If you get nothing else out of this book, it's essential that you heed and remember this Message – the Good News of Jesus Christ.

APPENDIX B:
WHERE CAN I LEARN MORE?

For further study on the men and women of the Bible, there are many resources available. The best is still a good Bible. You'll want to purchase one with a commentary which can explain some of the more difficult passages and help you understand everything in its proper context. I suggest either the Concordia Self Study Bible (NIV) or the Lutheran Study Bible (ESV), both of which contain concise and practical commentaries. The New International Version (NIV), English Standard Version (ESV), and the New King James Version (NKJV) are all excellent English translations of the Bible from the original Greek. An interesting book that I can recommend to you is Jaroslav Vajda's *Men and Women of the Word*. This book has wonderful snippets on over forty of the Bible's heavy hitters. While his emphasis is very different from my own, you can access a great amount of knowledge from such a book. I suggest you browse around in your own local bookstore or library and see what is available.

What I love most about this subject of "ordinary" people doing extraordinary things is that there is no shortage of examples from our own lives. Hollywood has made a fortune in movies about these sorts of people. However, the best examples are still those men and women in the church throughout the years who have helped to keep us on track in our faith and to preserve the purity of our beliefs. Even before the year 400 A.D., St. Augustine of Hippo was forming the foundational confessions of the Christian church as a whole. His revolutionary methods of catechesis and rhetoric shaped the way we catechize (teach) in our church even today. More recently, in the early 16th century, a monk named Martin Luther nailed his *95 Theses* to the Castle church door, signifying a future split in the church so that Protestant Christians (all Christians who aren't Roman Catholic) could worship in a way more congruent with the Bible. This isn't "anything goes" religion, but deeply Biblical and rooted in the Word of our Lord and Savior Jesus Christ. Great men such as John Calvin and Philip Melanchthon also helped see this movement to its completion. We know the congregations who came from this mindset better as the Lutherans, the Presbyterians, and the Reformed Church, from which the Baptists eventually came, not to mention hundreds of smaller congregations that are too numerous to mention. A couple hundred years after Luther and Calvin came men such as John Wesley, Jonathan Edwards, and George Whitefield. While these men may not be as familiar to you, their efforts shaped the quality of modern preaching and teaching, as well as modern scholarship and hymnody in the church. John Wesley's followers are better known as the Methodists, one of the largest Christian denominations in the world, having several branches in the United States alone and constituting several million members.

Why should you be interested in the stories of men from centuries ago who have nothing to do with you? Well, if you go to church, they have a lot to do with you. These men, along with many others worthy of mention, shaped the church into what it is today. Furthermore, most of them were born into situations that wouldn't have typically enabled them to accomplish such great feats. It was only through toil, perseverance, and faith that they shaped the world. They were sinners, every one of them, but God had a purpose for them just like He has a purpose for you and me. We should never think that the accounts in the Bible are just stories. They are an accurate portrayal for what happens in society even today. The wisdom of the Bible is timeless, and its examples carry on in our own lives as well.

Also from Tri-Pillar Publishing

TIMELY REFLECTIONS

A MINUTE A DAY WITH DALE MEYER

by Dale A. Meyer

*A minute's worth of reading
for a day's worth of reflection*

Timely Reflections is a collection of 365 inspirational devotions from the long-running and ever-popular Meyer Minute weekday online series. Dr. Meyer aptly uses Scripture – along with his own wisdom and experience – to guide his readers through the joys and pitfalls of daily living. Insightful, uplifting, and sometimes challenging, these daily reflections will provide plenty of spiritual food for thought. Set aside a minute a day to read, reflect, savor, and share each one!

Dr. Dale A. Meyer currently serves as President of
Concordia Seminary in St. Louis, MO.

$19.95 – Order online at www.tripillarpublishing.com

MEETING ANANIAS

AND OTHER EYE-OPENING STORIES OF FAITH

by James Tino
Foreword by Dale A. Meyer

Bring your faith back into focus!

Are you finding it harder to keep your faith energized? Why does the Christian life, initially so exciting and full of promise, often become routine and ordinary? It is easy to get overwhelmed by the concerns of life and to focus on the wrong things, which quickly drains the life out of our faith. We need to have our vision adjusted by the Word of God and the Holy Spirit so we can see the hand of God at work in our lives. In Meeting Ananias, our eyes are opened to see what we sometimes miss: the ordinary and extraordinary ways that God makes Himself known to us as we follow Him.

Rev. Dr. James Tino is Director of Global Lutheran Outreach,
a Lutheran mission-sending organization.

$11.95 – Order online at www.tripillarpublishing.com

MISSIONAL U

Life As a Mission Trip

DR. JACOB YOUMANS

Missional Living 101!

Trips to the mission field always bring new spiritual growth and insight to our lives. What if we could learn to see mission not as an event to take part in, but as a lifestyle to embrace? In *Missional U: Life As a Mission Trip*, that's exactly what Dr. Jacob Youmans teaches us as he shows, through Scripture and by personal example, what missional living is all about! If you're looking for a new way to travel, then come along. Missional U is your ticket to an exciting and fulfilling spiritual adventure – one that's sure to last a lifetime!

Dr. Jacob Youmans, a dynamic conference speaker, is Director of the DCE Program at Concordia University in Austin, Texas.

$14.95 – Order online at www.tripillarpublishing.com

MISSIONAL TOO

The Trip of a Lifetime

DR. JACOB YOUMANS

Bon Voyage... Again!

In this second volume of devotions on the joy of missional living, Dr. Jacob Youmans shows us what it means to see the world through redemptive eyes, love the world with an evangelistic heart, and travel the world with the Gospel of peace firmly on our feet. In Missional Too: The Trip of a Lifetime, we discover that when we walk in the footsteps of Jesus, the imprint we leave behind is His, not our own – and that makes all the difference. Our journey here as God's dearly loved people is a Gospel-sharing, disciple-making one.

Dr. Jacob Youmans, a dynamic conference speaker, is Director of the DCE Program at Concordia University in Austin, Texas.

$14.95 – Order online at www.tripillarpublishing.com

Shaking Scripture

Grasping More of God's Word

Rev. Mark Manning

Shaking Scripture was written to help develop a hunger within you for God's Word. You will see how intriguing and interesting the Bible can be. You will be guided through some of the well-known stories we've grown to love and that have, perhaps, gotten stale with familiarity. In addition, you will discover some lesser-known stories that just might surprise you because of their readability and application. In all, there are 12 devotions, each aimed at "Shaking Scripture" in a way that helps us grasp more of God's Word. Several reflective questions per devotion are also provided, making this book ideal for individual or group study.

Rev. Mark Manning serves as the pastor of Searchlight Ministries of Orange County, CA, where he shares his passion for understanding Scripture.

$14.95 – Order online at www.tripillarpublishing.com

Abba Daddy Do

exploration s in child like faith

by Dr. Jacob Youmans

Join the adventure of childlike faith!

When you're a child, every day is an adventure! Each day you see and experience life for the very first time. Reclaim the wonder and excitement meant for followers of Jesus as we explore the gift of childlike faith. Jacob Youmans, father of two, walks us through 40 true-life stories, discovering the spiritual in the everyday moments of childhood. Complete with study questions and scriptural references, this book is perfect for the individual looking to grow and be challenged, as well as a family or Bible study group.

Dr. Jacob Youmans, a dynamic conference speaker, is Director of the DCE Program at Concordia University in Austin, Texas.

$14.95 – Order online at www.tripillarpublishing.com

Powerful Love

An Introduction to Christianity

by Rev. Dr. Lloyd Strelow

You've got questions -
God's love provides the answers!

Powerful Love gets to the core of the essence of our Christian faith. The first chapter opens the window to God's love for each of us. It is through that window - guided by the Holy Spirit - that Christians see, believe, and live the rest of God's Word. Throughout Powerful Love, Pastor Strelow uses the inductive method, using our questions to lead us to search God's Word and find His answers for faith and life. Written as a basic guide to the Christian faith, Powerful Love also includes thoughtful study questions and an introductory guide

Rev. Dr. Lloyd Strelow has served six congregations in Michigan and California, including Prince of Peace Lutheran Church (LCMS) in Hemet, CA, where one of his primary emphases was to teach the basics of the Christian faith to all who seek to know the Lord.

$12.95 – Order online at www.tripillarpublishing.com

†ALKING PICTURES

How to turn a trip to the
movies into a mission trip

by Dr. Jacob Youmans
Foreword by Leonard Sweet

Movies and ministry? What's the story?

Movies are everywhere - at the theater, at home, on our computers, even in our pockets! Our culture's fascination with the power of movies brings us together in a shared experience. But did you ever think that watching the latest action-adventure flick with a friend could provide a truly unique opportunity to witness about your Christian faith? Talking Pictures examines the power of movies in our culture and explores effective ways in which we can use any movie as a way to start conversations about our Christian faith.

Dr. Jacob Youmans, a dynamic conference speaker, is Director of the DCE Program at Concordia University in Austin, Texas.

$14.95 – Order online at www.tripillarpublishing.com

Peter Dibble, digital artist

Graphic Design
Logos & Branding
Web Design
Video Production
Multimedia

Let us help design banners, brochures, etc.
for your church or organization.

www.peterwjdibble.com